"A timely and well-written book on [illegible]
reminds us that Christian theologiar[illegible]
most as servants of the Great Comm[illegible] much of the
Christian academy has been divorced from the gospel mission. The Bible is a theological, pastoral, and evangelistic book—and those must never be separated, lest one become malformed. I am immediately using this book with our elder and pastoral team!"

J. D. Greear, President, Southern Baptist Convention; author, *Not God Enough*; Pastor, The Summit Church, Raleigh-Durham, North Carolina

"Gavin Ortlund is a scholar and leader who both wields the sword of the Spirit and exhibits the fruit of the Spirit. He not only stands up for Jesus but also stands with him in love, holiness, and mission. In a sadly contentious time, this book shows us how to love each other and stay on mission together even when we see some nonessential doctrines in different ways. This is a wise and needed book."

Russell Moore, President, The Ethics & Religious Liberty Commission of the Southern Baptist Convention

"To put it simply: this is an important book. With a historian's insight, a theologian's precision, and a pastor's wisdom, Gavin Ortlund has given the church an invaluable handbook for navigating our ongoing doctrinal challenges and for healing our ongoing doctrinal divisions."

Jared C. Wilson, Assistant Professor of Pastoral Ministry, Spurgeon College; Author in Residence, Midwestern Baptist Theological Seminary; author, *The Imperfect Disciple*

"Some seem to think that faithfulness to God is measured in how much we argue about things. I am so grateful for Gavin Ortlund's book, which reminds us that faithfulness can be defined in far more biblical ways. Ortlund does not pretend that he has the answers to end all church arguments, but he helps us understand that failure to distinguish critical matters from secondary and tertiary concerns is an abandonment of the pastoral prudence that is essential to Christ's mission. Even Jesus said, 'I still have many things to say to you, but you cannot bear them now.' For pastors operating with the care and courage of Jesus, patience is not compromise, kindness is not weakness, and Christ's mission supersedes our personal victories. Ortlund honors Christ's manner as well as his message in this fascinating and challenging book."

Bryan Chapell, Pastor, Grace Presbyterian Church, Peoria, Illinois

"There are few needs today as urgent as the one Gavin Ortlund so ably addresses in this wonderful book. Healthy theological perspective and poise are all too absent in an age of immediate escalation and rage. This book could transform our thinking, our capacity for fellowship, and our witness to the world. I pray it is read widely and heeded deeply."

Sam Allberry, author, *Why Does God Care Who I Sleep With?* and *7 Myths about Singleness*

"Gavin Ortlund helps us think well as brothers and sisters in Christ on where we must staunchly defend the truth and draw immovable lines. He also helps us know where to extend grace and lovingly disagree while working together for the fulfillment of the Great Commission and the building up of the Lord's church. This book is much needed in our day. May our Savior use it for our good and his glory."

Daniel L. Akin, President, Southeastern Baptist Theological Seminary

"In this age of theological infighting and compromise, Gavin Ortlund issues a clarion call for wisdom. You don't have to agree with him on everything to appreciate his sane and clarifying advice. This is an important book for our time, helping the church as we struggle for both faithfulness to God's word and a proper Christian unity."

Michael Reeves, President and Professor of Theology, Union School of Theology, Oxford, United Kingdom

"As best I can tell, this is the first book of its kind and is long overdue. Gavin Ortlund has done the church a tremendous service by providing a clear, irenic, and well-reasoned (not to mention biblical) perspective on the comparative importance of our many Christian doctrines. Some in the church today have waged vigorous war and 'died' needlessly on virtually every hill, while others, in the name of unity, don't find any hill worth 'dying' on. To both, and to everyone in between the two extremes, I say, 'Read this book!'"

Sam Storms, Senior Pastor, Bridgeway Church, Oklahoma City, Oklahoma

FINDING THE RIGHT HILLS TO DIE ON

Other Gospel Coalition Books

Christ Has Set Us Free: Preaching and Teaching Galatians, edited by D. A. Carson and Jeff Robinson Sr.

Coming Home: Essays on the New Heaven and New Earth, edited by D. A. Carson and Jeff Robinson Sr.

Confronting Christianity: 12 Hard Questions for the World's Largest Religion, by Rebecca McLaughlin

Don't Call It a Comeback: The Old Faith for a New Day, edited by Kevin DeYoung

Faithful Endurance: The Joy of Shepherding People for a Lifetime, edited by Collin Hansen and Jeff Robinson Sr.

15 Things Seminary Couldn't Teach Me, edited by Collin Hansen and Jeff Robinson

Glory in the Ordinary: Why Your Work in the Home Matters to God, by Courtney Reissig

God's Love Compels Us: Taking the Gospel to the World, edited by D. A. Carson and Kathleen B. Nielson

God's Word, Our Story: Learning from the Book of Nehemiah, edited by D. A. Carson and Kathleen B. Nielson

The Gospel as Center: Renewing Our Faith and Reforming Our Ministry Practices, edited by D. A. Carson and Timothy Keller

Gospel-Centered Youth Ministry: A Practical Guide, edited by Cameron Cole and Jon Nielson

Here Is Our God: God's Revelation of Himself in Scripture, edited by Kathleen B. Nielson and D. A. Carson

His Mission: Jesus in the Gospel of Luke, edited by D. A. Carson and Kathleen B. Nielson

Joyfully Spreading the Word, edited by Kathleen Nielson and Gloria Furman

Missional Motherhood, by Gloria Furman

The New City Catechism: 52 Questions and Answers for Our Hearts and Minds

The New City Catechism Curriculum

The New City Catechism Devotional: God's Truth for Our Hearts and Minds

The New City Catechism for Kids

The Pastor as Scholar and the Scholar as Pastor: Reflections on Life and Ministry, by John Piper and D. A. Carson, edited by David Mathis and Owen Strachan

Praying Together: The Priority and Privilege of Prayer: In Our Homes, Communities, and Churches, by Megan Hill

Pursuing Health in an Anxious Age, by Bob Cutillo

Remember Death, by Matthew McCullough

Resurrection Life in a World of Suffering, edited by D. A. Carson and Kathleen Nielson

FINDING THE RIGHT HILLS TO DIE ON

The Case for Theological Triage

Gavin Ortlund

Foreword by D. A. Carson

WHEATON, ILLINOIS

Finding the Right Hills to Die On: The Case for Theological Triage

Published by Crossway
1300 Crescent Street
Wheaton, Illinois 60187

Cover design: Jordan Singer

Cover image: Sheet 62Dd SW, 1:20000, GSGS 2742, April 1918 (colour litho), English School, (20th century) / National Army Museum, London / Bridgeman Images

First printing 2020

Printed in the United States of America

All emphases in Scripture quotations have been added by the author.

Trade paperback ISBN: 978-1-4335-6742-1
ePub ISBN: 978-1-4335-6745-2
PDF ISBN: 978-1-4335-6743-8
Mobipocket ISBN: 978-1-4335-6744-5

Library of Congress Cataloging-in-Publication Data

Names: Ortlund, Gavin, 1983– author.
Title: Finding the right hills to die on: the case for theological triage / Gavin Ortlund; foreword by D. A. Carson.
Description: Wheaton, Illinois: Crossway, 2020. | Series: The gospel coalition | Includes bibliographical references and index.
Identifiers: LCCN 2019041185 (print) | LCCN 2019041186 (ebook) | ISBN 9781433567421 (trade paperback) | ISBN 9781433567438 (pdf) | ISBN 9781433567445 (mobipocket) | ISBN 9781433567452 (epub)
Subjects: LCSH: Theology, Doctrinal. | Pastoral theology. | Christian leadership. | Church work.
Classification: LCC BT78 .O7835 2020 (print) | LCC BT78 (ebook) | DDC 230—dc23
LC record available at https://lccn.loc.gov/2019041185
LC ebook record available at https://lccn.loc.gov/2019041186

Crossway is a publishing ministry of Good News Publishers.

VP 33 32 31 30 29 28 27 26 25 24
17 16 15 14 13 12 11 10 9 8 7 6

To Covenant Theological Seminary
and Immanuel Church, Nashville,
two institutions that display beauty
in their theological culture

Contents

Foreword

Some years ago I watched with interest as a senior minister I greatly admired resigned from his ministry in Canada and left to serve in France. He already spoke French with some fluency, and he was greatly stirred by the smallness and low number of evangelical churches in that country. So, not long before the age when many people would have been dreaming of retirement, he felt called of God to address this great need, and off he went.

He lasted just over thirty months before he was asked to leave by the same group of evangelical churches that had warmly invited him to come and help them.

About the same time, I got to know a youngish man who became a missionary to a Slavic country that could have certainly used his help. He too was asked to leave. He lasted less than two years.

The first man had come from a North American denomination that was adamantly opposed to the use of alcohol by Christians. Believing this stance was morally right, he tried to convince his French brothers and sisters in Christ of the rightness of this position. From their point of view, not only was he wrong, but, even if they could imagine he might be right, they felt he was making a mountain out of a molehill. He dug in and brought up the subject so frequently that pretty soon his position became untenable.

The second man came from a freewheeling North American denomination from which he had derived many of his ethical practices (one hesitates to call them principles). The Slavic brothers and sisters in Christ found him to be loose and undisciplined: imagine going to mixed swimming sites! That's what unbelievers do, exposing acres of bare flesh and undermining Christian efforts to follow the ways of chastity and holiness. Sadly, he interpreted their stance as interfering with his Christian freedom, and pretty soon he was urged to return to California.

Both of these examples deal with something not directly addressed by Gavin Ortlund, namely, the challenges of cross-cultural church practices, cross-cultural codes of conduct, cross-cultural communication. Nevertheless, behind these issues lies a still larger issue, the issue that Dr. Ortlund powerfully tackles in this insightful and probing book. It is the issue of *theological triage*.

As far as I know, the expression "theological triage" was first coined by R. Albert Mohler, who draws analogies with medical triage. At the scene of a terrible accident or some other violent event, there may be too few first responders to deal with all the victims immediately. Decisions have to be made: should the first concentrated attention go to the victim with severe burns, the victim who is bleeding profusely, or the victim with a couple of broken limbs? It is the responsibility of the initial triage teams to make these hard choices. Similarly, in the realm of theology some theological issues are more important or more urgent than others, and Christians who have to decide on how best to deploy their energy need to exercise godly judgment as to where their theological priorities should go.

Ortlund usefully develops four tiers in his theological-triage system: (1) doctrines that are *essential* to the gospel; (2) doctrines that are *urgent* for the health and practice of the church, such that Christians commonly divide denominationally over them; (3) doctrines that are *important* for one branch of theology or another, but not such that they should lead to separation; (4) doctrines that are *unimportant* to gospel witness and ministry collaboration.

Of course, some believers distance themselves from such triage grids. If the Bible asserts something, they avow, it is God's truth and not to be relativized or declared more (or less) important than any other part of God's truth. Others resort to what might be called "LCD theology" (Lowest Common Denominator theology). The question that interests them is this: What is the *least* that any person should believe and adhere to in order to be a Christian? Both of these strategies will readily dismiss all attempts at theological triage.

It is precisely here that Ortlund is a helpful guide. He helpfully points out that Paul (to go no further) can designate certain doctrines as matters "of first importance" (1 Cor. 15:3), while other beliefs allow for difference of opinion (Rom. 14:5). Certainly when the apostle finds himself in different cultural settings, he feels free to emphasize slightly different things as he takes his audience into account (compare his sermons in Acts 13 and Acts 17 respectively, one in a synagogue and one in the Areopagus). This book seeks to establish clear thinking about such questions. When he comes to concrete examples, Ortlund is less eager that you should agree with all his conclusions than that you learn how to think about the importance of theological triage. And this becomes all the more important when theological triage is overlaid with the challenges of cross-cultural communication.

This book is a little exercise on how to read and use your Bible humbly, carefully, faithfully, and wisely, like workers who do not need to be ashamed.

D. A. Carson

Acknowledgments

One of my goals in this book was to write with a sensitivity to the real issues affecting local churches. So I conducted a number of interviews with various pastors in order to learn how different doctrines have played out in their ministries. I want to express my appreciation for the insights of Brad Andrews, Jeremiah Hurt, J. A. Medders, Ben Vrbicek, Simon Murphy, and Hans Kristensen. Kristensen and Murphy were particularly helpful in giving a sense of the scene in Australia and Singapore, where they respectively minister.

I am grateful to Collin Hansen and Jeff Robinson for the invitation to write this book and their collaboration along the way. Greg Strand offered helpful feedback as well. Justin Taylor and Andy Naselli directed me to several helpful resources. The entire team at Crossway did, as always, an incredible job. Special thanks to Thom Notaro for his careful editing.

Introduction

There's an old saying (I can't remember where I heard it): "There is no doctrine a fundamentalist *won't* fight over, and no doctrine a liberal *will* fight over." Strictly speaking, that's not quite fair to thoughtful liberals and fundamentalists. But we can probably recognize these two instincts. Most of us have a tendency in one direction or the other—to fight over doctrine too much or too little.

This book is about finding the happy place between these two extremes—the place of wisdom, love, and courage that will best serve the church and advance the gospel in our fractured times. In other words, it's about finding the right hills to die on.

Albert Mohler has developed a helpful metaphor for this idea: *theological triage*.[1] Triage is essentially a system of prioritization. It is often used in medical contexts. For instance, if you are a doctor on the battlefield, you cannot treat every wounded soldier simultaneously, so you must develop a process to determine which injuries you treat first.

Using the concept of triage in the context of theology assumes two things. First, doctrines have different kinds of importance. Some hills are worth dying on. Others are not. As basic as this might seem, plenty of people, either in principle

1. For instance, see R. Albert Mohler Jr., *The Disappearance of God: Dangerous Beliefs in the New Spiritual Openness* (Colorado Springs: Multnomah, 2009), 1–8.

or in practice, deny this—more on that in a moment. Second, triage assumes that the needs are urgent. You can spend more time fixing a broken arm when no one is hemorrhaging ten feet away. If you have neither a broken arm nor a dying man to attend to, you can give more attention to a chipped tooth or bad bruise. But the more demanding the issues, the more you have to make hard decisions.

Similarly, if souls were not perishing, if our culture were not seeming to escalate into a whirlwind of confusion and outrage, if the church did not have so many languishing needs—I suppose, if these were not the conditions we faced, we could do away with theological triage and work on every doctrine all at once. But the dire needs of the times require us to make strategic decisions of prioritization in order to be as effective as possible at pleasing Christ, serving the church, and advancing his gospel.

Now, everyone understands how important triage is in a medical context. Just think what would happen if you didn't have triage! One person would lose a limb so another could have his arm set. In the worst scenario, one person would die so another could have a bruise bandaged.

But we often forget to think in the same way about theology. Sometimes we flatten out all doctrine—either because we want to fight about everything or because we want to fight about nothing. More commonly, we have some kind of functional theological triage, but we have not thought it through very self-consciously. As a result, it is determined reactively by our circumstances and temperament rather than proactively by Scripture and principle.

There are all kinds of ways to distinguish doctrines.[2] In this book I suggest four basic categories. We could explore further

2. Erik Thoennes, *Life's Biggest Questions: What the Bible Says about the Things That Matter Most* (Wheaton, IL: Crossway, 2011), 35, suggests a similar fourfold categorization: "Absolutes define the core beliefs of the Christian faith; convictions, while not

subcategories as well, but this fourfold ranking should help as a starting point:

- First-rank doctrines are *essential* to the gospel itself.
- Second-rank doctrines are *urgent* for the health and practice of the church such that they frequently cause Christians to separate at the level of local church, denomination, and/or ministry.
- Third-rank doctrines are *important* to Christian theology, but not enough to justify separation or division among Christians.
- Fourth-rank doctrines are *unimportant* to our gospel witness and ministry collaboration.

In this book I consider the Trinity, for example, to be a first-rank doctrine, baptism a second-rank doctrine, and the millennium a third-rank doctrine (more about that later). An older term, borrowed from Greek, that roughly corresponds to category 4 is *adiaphora*, literally meaning "things indifferent." In Lutheran and Puritan circles, this term was used to identify practices or views that are neither commanded nor forbidden by Scripture. An example of a fourth-rank issue is the musical instrumentation used in worship or the number of angels that exist. Fourth-rank issues might be practically relevant or intellectually stimulating, but they are not *theologically* important.

core beliefs, may have significant impact on the health and effectiveness of the church; opinions are less-clear issues that generally are not worth dividing over; and questions are currently unsettled issues." Another gradation is dogma, doctrine, and opinions (Roger E. Olson, *The Mosaic of Christian Belief: Twenty Centuries of Unity and Diversity* [Downers Grove, IL: InterVarsity Press, 2002], 44). Daniel B. Wallace, "My Take on Inerrancy," Bible.org, August 10, 2006, https://bible.org/article/my-take-inerrancy, provides a helpful and slightly more nuanced list of four kinds of doctrines (italics his):

1. What doctrines are essential for the *life* of the church?
2. What doctrines are important for the *health* of the church?
3. What doctrines are distinctives that are necessary for the *practice* of the local church?
4. What doctrines belong to the *speculative* realm or should never divide the church?

Not everything will fit neatly into one of these four categories, of course.[3] But at least they provide a basic framework from which we can make further specifications and nuances as necessary.

You might be interested in this book if you have wrestled with questions like these:

- How do we pursue the realization of Christ's prayer for the unity of the church (John 17:21) without disobeying Christ's charge to obey all that he commands (Matt. 28:20)?
- What partnerships and alliances are appropriate among Christians of different denominations, networks, or tribes?
- What kinds of attitude and speech are most helpful in our interaction with those in the body of Christ with whom we have significant theological disagreements?
- What does it look like to handle, with integrity and transparency, personal differences of conviction that may arise with your church, boss, denomination, or institution?

Or, perhaps you can relate to one of the following fictional scenarios:

1. You are relatively new on the pastoral staff at a local church. In a particular song the congregation is accustomed to singing, you have a reservation about some of the lyrics. You wonder whether it's a big enough deal to address and, if so, how soon in your time at the church you should tackle this, and what the process and communication should be like.

---

3. I first articulated this fourfold schema in my article "When Should Doctrine Divide?," The Gospel Coalition, August 14, 2017, https://www.thegospelcoalition.org/article/when-should-doctrine-divide. Some of the material here expands upon this article, as well as my prior article "3 Reflections on Cultivating Theological Poise," The Gospel Coalition, August 10, 2015, https://www.thegospelcoalition.org/article/cultivating-an-ethos-of-poise.

2. You have been working at a parachurch ministry for several years. As part of your contract, you have to annually reaffirm your commitment to the statement of faith of the denomination with which the ministry is associated. The statement of faith affirms a particular view of the end times that you had not studied much when you took the job, and you were happy at that time to affirm it. Over the years, however, you've grown unsettled about this view, and at this point you lean away from it, though you are not fully decided. You hesitate to keep studying it, for fear of landing in a place that threatens your job. In your conscience, you wonder at what point you need to communicate your reservations about this doctrine. Is it only when you have fully decided? If so, what does this process look like, and how do you go about it?

3. A group of churches in your community is putting on a joint service of worship and outreach. You have significant theological differences with some of the other churches participating, and you wonder whether you can take part with a good conscience. How do you decide what to do? And what does it look like to approach this situation with graciousness and humility without compromising your convictions?

4. You love listening to a particular Bible preacher on the radio. His sermons are both convicting and uplifting. But one day you learn that he speaks at conferences that have a "health and wealth" emphasis, and you start to notice aspects of his teaching that can be interpreted in this way. How should your perception of his preaching be altered (if at all) by his broader ministry associations? How clearly must his own teaching veer into a "health and wealth" gospel before you stop listening?

5. You are dating seriously and thinking about marriage. However, you and your companion hold different views on the proper expression of gender roles within a marriage. You

have talked through the issues with other trusted Christians and studied the question with your prospective spouse, but the two of you have not reached a resolution. Should you break up? How should you think about your differences?

These are some of the scenarios I have in mind while I write this book, though what we arrive at will hopefully be more than a series of "how to" answers to questions like these. Instead, we are after a set of theological instincts that can guide us in various situations of real life and ministry. Thus, the variety of issues addressed in this book are meant to be illustrative, not exhaustive.

Some of the doctrines I'll cover are ones I've personally agonized over, like creation and baptism. But I want to make it clear up front that my desire in this book is not to convert you to my view on these doctrines (really, I mean that). Rather, I'm trying to get at the whole way we go about theology, in both forming our convictions and then navigating life and ministry in light of them. I sincerely hope that this book will help you as you form your *own* convictions about how theological triage should function in your life and ministry.

I'm writing from an evangelical Protestant perspective, and I draw particularly from resources within the Reformed tradition. Nonetheless, the principles and topics covered here have a broad relevance, and I'd be delighted if Christians from other traditions, or non-Christians, found value in this book.

One note of caution: some of the most divisive issues among Christians concern not theological matters per se but cultural, wisdom, and political issues. For example, should Christians send their children to public schools or private schools or do home schooling? Under what circumstances, if any, may Christians drink alcohol? When and how (if at all) should reference to current political and cultural events be made in a church service? These are all important questions, but in this book I am focusing more on specifically theological matters.

In the first two chapters, then, I will identify two opposite errors to provide an overall framework for thinking about the importance of doctrine. Then, in chapter 3, I want to share a little bit of my story. This will help explain how this whole topic came up for me and why I think it is so important. It will also start to get us into specific doctrines. Chapters 4–6 will work through a number of specific doctrines in light of theological triage, attempting to identify criteria for ranking the importance of different issues.

PART 1

WHY THEOLOGICAL TRIAGE?

1

The Danger of Doctrinal Sectarianism

It is easy to lose your balance when you're standing on one foot. The strongest posture is one of balance between both feet: one of *poise*. That's why boxers put so much care into their footwork.

In our theological life as well, we need poise. The character of the gospel is complex. It contains both truth and grace, both conviction and comfort, both hard edges of logic and deep caverns of mystery. It is at one moment as bracing as a cold breeze and the next as nourishing as a warm meal. Faithfulness to the gospel, therefore, requires more than one virtue. We must at times boldly contend and at other times gently probe. In one situation we must emphasize what is obvious, and in another we must explore what is nuanced.

Jesus is the perfect blend of these diverse qualities—"gentle and lowly in heart" (Matt. 11:29) and yet unafraid to cleanse the temple (Matt. 21:12–13) or denounce the Pharisees (Matt. 23). Most of us, by contrast, tend to tilt toward *either* courage *or* gentleness, particularly when it comes to theological disagreement. For instance, we might be naturally careful about theological clarity but have a blind spot to the destructiveness of divisiveness. In the other direction, we might be horrified at the lack of love some Christians exhibit but naive about the effects of doctrinal erosion. As Martin Luther noted, "Softness and hardness . . . are the two main faults from which all the mistakes of pastors come."[1] The same could be said of all Christians.

This chapter therefore addresses the danger of doctrinal sectarianism, and the following chapter addresses its opposite, the danger of doctrinal minimalism. By doctrinal sectarianism I mean any attitude, belief, or practice that contributes to unnecessary division in the body of Christ. Doctrinal sectarianism often results from the inability to distinguish between different kinds of doctrine. So we must begin by asking what rationale we have to make such distinctions in the first place.

Are All Doctrines Created Equal?

People often claim that "all sins are the same in God's eyes." That sounds spiritual because it seems to take sin seriously. And it is certainly true that any sin is enough to make us guilty before a holy God. For instance, James 2:10 says that "whoever keeps the whole law but fails in one point has become guilty of all of it."

But on closer examination, there is much in the Bible that would discourage us from considering all sins equal. The prophets decried some sins as more heinous than others (Jer. 16:12; Ezek. 23:11). Jesus spoke of "the weightier matters of the law" (Matt. 23:23) and of lesser and greater degrees of punishment for different kinds of sin (Matt. 10:15; Luke 12:47–48; John

1. Martin Luther, *Luther's Works*, vol. 25, *Lectures on Romans* (St. Louis: Concordia, 1972), 139.

19:11). The Old Testament law made provision for different kinds of sins, such as "unintentional" versus "high-handed" sins (Num. 15:22–31). First John 5:16–17 distinguishes "sin that leads to death" from other sins. As the Westminster Shorter Catechism explains, "Some sins in themselves, and by reason of several aggravations, are more heinous in the sight of God than others."[2]

In an analogous way, it might initially sound good to say that "all *doctrines* are equally important," but it is a difficult statement to justify biblically. Paul, for instance, speaks of the gospel as a matter of "first importance" (1 Cor. 15:3). On other topics, he often gives Christians greater latitude to disagree. For instance, in Philippians 3:15 he writes, "If in anything you think otherwise, God will reveal that also to you." On certain issues, he goes further and commands Christians not to "quarrel over opinions" (Rom. 14:1). Even on an important topic like baptism, Paul draws a prioritization for the gospel: "Christ did not send me to baptize but to preach the gospel" (1 Cor. 1:17).

Why is it important to make doctrinal distinctions? What is at stake? For starters, equating all doctrines leads to unnecessary division and undermines the unity of the church.

Unnecessary Division Harms the Unity of the Church

Historically, theologians in the Reformed tradition have often drawn a distinction between essential and nonessential beliefs out of concern for the unity of the church. Writing in the seventeenth century, Francis Turretin provided a series of arguments that certain "fundamental articles" are more important than others.[3] As he put it, some doctrines are "primary and

2. The Shorter Catechism, Q. 83, in *The Westminster Confession of Faith* (Glasgow: Free Presbyterian, 1966), 309–10.

3. Francis Turretin, *Institutes of Elenctic Theology*, trans. George Musgrave Giger, ed. James T. Dennison Jr., 3 vols. (Phillipsburg, NJ: P&R, 1992–1997), 1.14.1–27.

immediate; such as the articles concerning the Trinity, Christ the Mediator, justification, etc.," while others are "secondary and mediate," and come into view only as a consequence of these primary doctrines.[4] Turretin also observed that different doctrines serve different functions. Some doctrines are necessary to produce faith; others are necessary to perfect and grow faith.[5] To support this observation, he drew attention to the distinction between milk and solid food in Hebrews 5:12–14. He saw solid food as a metaphor for more established and nuanced doctrines, and milk as a metaphor for "the basic principles of the oracles of God" (v. 12).

Turretin also maintained that there are different kinds of theological errors, with corresponding levels of severity. For instance, some errors are about doctrinal language or phrases only (he calls these "verbal errors"); others are about the doctrines themselves (he calls these "real errors").[6] Additionally, we can be in error about the substance of a doctrine or in error about its mode and circumstances. As an example, Turretin argued that the Greeks (those whom we often call Eastern Orthodox) are in error about the mode of the procession of the Holy Spirit but that this does not constitute an error about the Trinity itself or the divinity of the Spirit.[7]

Why was it so important for Turretin to distinguish between different kinds of doctrine and different kinds of error? In his own context, Turretin was facing two distinct threats. First, he was concerned by Socinian and Roman Catholic claims that their distinctive doctrines were fundamental truths of the faith. But, second, Turretin was concerned about other orthodox Protestant traditions that were dividing over nonessential mat-

4. Turretin, *Institutes*, 1.14.8.
5. Turretin, *Institutes*, 1.14.7.
6. Turretin, *Institutes*, 1.14.12.
7. Turretin, *Institutes*, 1.14.15.

ters of doctrine. In other words, Turretin was opposing not only the elevation of what he regarded as *false* doctrines into necessary articles of faith but also the elevation of *true but secondary* doctrines into necessary articles of faith. This concerned Turretin because it led to unnecessary separation among true Christians. For instance, he faulted "the more strict Lutherans who (to render a union with us more difficult) extend fundamentals more widely than is just, turn almost every error into a heresy, and make necessary those things which are indifferent."[8] Here it is evident that Turretin's concern about elevating nonfundamental doctrines to a fundamental status derives from a deeper concern about the unity of the church. The problem with making every error a heresy is that it "renders union more difficult."

The Protestant Reformer John Calvin voiced a similar concern. In his famous *Institutes of the Christian Religion*, Calvin warned against the error of "capricious separation" from true churches and Christians. He argued that what marks a true church is "the pure ministry of the word and pure mode of celebrating the sacraments." If a church possesses these marks, "we must not reject it so long as it retains them, even if it otherwise swarms with many faults."[9] Calvin further allowed that there may be errors in the *way* a church practices these two marks, and yet it is a true church: "Some faults may creep into the administration of either doctrine or sacraments, but this ought not to estrange us from communion with the church."[10] But how do we know which errors are severe enough to require us to separate from a particular church? Calvin developed an answer to this dilemma by appealing to a distinction between primary and secondary doctrines:

8. Turretin, *Institutes*, 1.14.2.
9. John Calvin, *Institutes of the Christian Religion*, ed. John T. McNeill, trans. Ford Lewis Battles, 2 vols. (Louisville: Westminster John Knox, 2006), 4.1.12.
10. Calvin, *Institutes*, 4.1.12.

> For not all the articles of true doctrine are of the same sort. Some are so necessary to know that they should be certain and unquestioned by all men as the proper principles of religion. Such are: God is one; Christ is God and the Son of God; our salvation rests in God's mercy; and the like. Among the churches there are other articles of doctrine disputed which still do not break the unity of faith.[11]

As an example of the latter kind of doctrine—those over which it is not necessary to break the unity of faith—Calvin identifies a difference of opinion among those who think that the souls of believers fly to heaven upon death, and those who would not dare to define the place to which souls go, but acknowledge that they live to the Lord. Citing Philippians 3:15, Calvin insists that such differences of opinion would not be a source of division apart from "unbridled contention and opinionated stubbornness."[12] He goes so far as to assert that churches will not survive apart from a willingness to tolerate errors on lesser matters:

> A difference of opinion over these nonessential matters should in no wise be the basis of schism among Christians. . . . Either we must leave no church remaining, or we must condone delusion in those matters which can go unknown without harm to the sum of religion and without loss of salvation.[13]

Calvin argued strenuously and at great length against the sin of schism, emphasizing that the church will always be mixed and imperfect until judgment day, and that much separatism comes from pride rather than holiness.[14]

11. Calvin, *Institutes*, 4.1.12.
12. Calvin, *Institutes*, 4.1.12.
13. Calvin, *Institutes*, 4.1.12. Where the Battles translation has "condone delusion," John Allen (1813) renders it "forgive mistakes."
14. Calvin, *Institutes*, 4.1.13–22.

The Unity of the Church Is Essential to the Mission of the Church

The concern Calvin and Turretin expressed about unnecessary division stemmed from the value they attached to the unity of the church. We should maintain this concern today. Some of us have a natural bent to worry about doctrinal minimalism. We are eager to "contend for the faith that was once for all delivered to the saints" (Jude 3), and we are on alert against any watering down of biblical truth in the face of cultural pressure. This is good, but we must be careful that we are not naive about how destructive sins in the opposite direction can be. It is false to think that doctrinal minimalism is necessarily or inherently more destructive than doctrinal sectarianism. Errors in both directions can diminish our gospel impact.

The unity of the church is not an optional add-on—something we can get to later, once we've gotten our doctrine straight. The church's unity is foundational to her identity and mission. For example, it is one of the four marks or attributes of the church recognized in the early creeds: *one, holy, catholic, and apostolic.* But what does it mean, exactly, to say that the church is *one*? How do we reconcile this affirmation with the divisions and rifts we see throughout church history and today?

To affirm the unity of the church is to affirm that there are not multiple, distinct groups that constitute separate peoples of God. Jesus does not have a plurality of brides. He has *one* bride, and her unity is so important that, as Paul stipulates in Ephesians 2:14, it was among the intended aims of Jesus's atoning death: "he . . . has made us both one and has broken down in his flesh the dividing wall of hostility." In context, Paul is speaking of the union of Jews and Gentiles, but his point is certainly relevant to all expressions of unity in the body of Christ, including among various estranged Gentile groups. Note the words *in his flesh*. It was at the cost of Jesus's death that we were reconciled to God and, in the same movement, reconciled with those reconciled to God. If we have peace with God, we have peace with each other. Our unity is so important that Jesus gave his blood for it.

If we value the cross, we should value the unity of the church. When Paul rebukes the factious Corinthians, he does so by pointing them to Jesus's death for them as the object of their ultimate allegiance: "Is Christ divided? Was Paul crucified for you?" (1 Cor. 1:13). Not only this, the unity of the church is ultimately grounded in the deeper reality of who God is. Later in Ephesians, Paul writes, "There is one body and one Spirit—just as you were called to the one hope that belongs to your call—one Lord, one faith, one baptism, one God and Father of all, who is over all and through all and in all" (Eph. 4:4–6; see also 1 Cor. 1:10–17). It is striking in this passage how Paul weaves together the church's unity (one body, hope, faith, and baptism) with God's triune unity (one Spirit, Lord, and God and Father). Martyn Lloyd-Jones suggested that Paul probably structured this passage in order to show that "the unity of the Church is a manifestation of the perfection of the Godhead."[15]

There are, of course, different expressions of Christian unity: being ordained in a particular denomination is one thing; becoming a member of a local church is another; attending a prayer meeting is another; and speaking at a conference is another. We should have lower theological criteria for looser forms of partnership. There are a range of nuances involved in knowing how to pursue unity in any given situation, and we cannot resolve every question here. But let me at least make one basic point: the unity of the church is essential to the *mission* of the church.

---

15. D. Martyn Lloyd-Jones, *Christian Unity: An Exposition of Ephesians 4:1–16* (Grand Rapids, MI: Baker, 1998), 49.

We see this, for instance, in John 17:21, where Jesus prays that those who believe in his name "may all be one, just as you, Father, are in me, and I in you, that they also may be in us, so that the world may believe that you have sent me." It is striking that Jesus correlates the kind of unity that Christians should experience with the unity he has with the Father. As followers of Jesus, we are called to be one with each other just as the Father is in the Son, and the Son is in the Father. And this unity serves a vital purpose for the church: "that the world may believe that you have sent me." When we think of the church's unity, we often think of her internal health—avoiding church splits and so forth. That is true, of course, but in this passage Jesus raises the stakes. The church's unity is essential to the advance of the gospel around us.

One does not need to be particularly well studied in church history to know that churches are not often known for their unity. Though estimates of the number of Protestant denominations are often exaggerated,[16] the fragmentation is undeniable. Thoughtful Protestants have always lamented this fact. The Dutch theologian Herman Bavinck, for example, commented that "the rise of sectarianism that has accompanied the Protestant movement is a dark and negative phenomenon."[17] In the context of his treatment of the church's catholicity (that is, universality), Bavinck stressed the importance of recognizing a distinction between fundamental and nonfundamental truths. He went so far as to claim that the inability to recognize true Christians outside one's own circle leads to the spiritual detriment and ultimately to the death of that group:

---

16. As an example of a higher estimate, see "Status of Global Christianity, 2019, in the Context of 1900–2050," https://gordonconwell.edu/center-for-global-christianity/resources/status-of-global-christianity/, accessed August 3, 2019. High-end estimates typically operate with a very loose definition of the term "denomination."

17. Herman Bavinck, "The Catholicity of Christianity and the Church," trans. John Bolt, *Calvin Theological Journal* 27 (1992): 247. I am grateful to Timothy Paul Jones for directing me to this article.

> No one church, no matter how pure, is identical with the universal church. In the same way no confession, no matter how refined by the Word of God, is identical with the whole of Christian truth. Each sect that considers its own circle as the only church of Christ and makes exclusive claims to truth will wither and die like a branch severed from its vine.[18]

It's not hard to see how this can happen. The results of unnecessary doctrinal division—church splits, aloofness from how God is at work in our city, failed opportunities to link arms with other ministries, and so on—are incredibly damaging to the mission of the church. Those who completely wall themselves off from other genuine Christians will not flourish. Within the body of Christ, we need each other—and often we especially need those Christians who lean in a different direction than we do. As Collin Hansen reminds us, seeing our own blind spots and learning to appreciate how God has gifted other Christians often run together:

> It's so easy to see the fault in someone else or in another group but so difficult to see the limitations in ourselves. Unless you learn to see the faults in yourself and your heroes, though, you can't appreciate how God has gifted other Christians. . . . Only then can we meet the challenges of our rapidly changing age.[19]

Pursuing the unity of the church does not mean that we should stop caring about theology. But it does mean that our love of theology should never exceed our love of real people, and therefore we must learn to love people amid our theo-

18. Bavinck, "Catholicity of Christianity and the Church," 250–51.
19. Collin Hansen, *Blind Spots: Becoming a Courageous, Compassionate, and Commissioned Church* (Wheaton, IL: Crossway, 2015), 26.

logical disagreements. As Spurgeon explained, talking about George Herbert:

> Where the Spirit of God is there must be love, and if I have once known and recognized any man to be my brother in Christ Jesus, the love of Christ constraineth me no more to think of him as a stranger or foreigner, but a fellow citizen with the saints. Now I hate High Churchism as my soul hates Satan; but I love George Herbert, although George Herbert is a desperately High Churchman. I hate his High Churchism, but I love George Herbert from my very soul, and I have a warm corner in my heart for every man who is like him. Let me find a man who loves my Lord Jesus Christ as George Herbert did and I do not ask myself whether I shall love him or not; there is no room for question, for I cannot help myself; unless I can leave off loving Jesus Christ, I cannot cease loving those who love him. . . . I will defy you, if you have any love to Jesus Christ, to pick or choose among His people.[20]

Do we have a "warm corner in our hearts" for every single true Christian, even if we strongly disagree with him or her on various issues? Spurgeon reminds us that if we love Jesus, we must love and embrace all those who belong to him. To leave off loving the people of Christ, as he put it, is to leave off loving Christ himself.

But loving all Christians is not easy to do! Some will inevitably annoy you, and the things some Christians believe and practice may deeply concern you (think of Spurgeon "hating" Herbert's High Churchism). Nonetheless, we cannot emotionally stiff-arm other members of the body of Christ. If we love Jesus, we must love those who belong to him.

20. Charles Spurgeon, sermon 668, "Unity in Christ," in *The Complete Works of C. H. Spurgeon*, vol. 12, *Sermons 668 to 727* (Cleveland, OH: Pilgrim, 2013).

Now, again, this love may not ultimately manifest in formal church membership together. There are different expressions of unity. And the healing of division in the church is complicated—where there have been real wounds, for instance, there may need to be confrontation and accountability. But we can start, at the very least, with the attitude of our hearts. Do we *want* unity? Is it a value to us, as it is to Jesus?

A good prayer to pray is this:

> Lord, give me a "warm corner in my heart" for other Christians, especially those I am tempted to reject or despise. I know that I cannot solve all the divisions in your church, but show me what the next step might be for me personally to pursue and cultivate and honor the unity of your bride.

Jesus will give us grace where we have failed and help us know how to move forward.

Quarreling about Unimportant Doctrines Harms the Godliness of the Church

We must go even further. Doctrinal sectarianism harms not only the unity and mission of the church but also the holiness of the church. Consider, for instance, the way Paul sets doctrinal priorities in the Pastoral Epistles. Through these letters Paul repeatedly warns both Timothy and Titus against getting involved in foolish disputes about myths, genealogies, and other speculative topics that certain persons are stirring up. It is striking how often Paul grounds his admonition in a desire for the *godliness* of the churches Titus and Timothy are serving. Consider the concerns Paul articulates in the following passages:

- "Remain at Ephesus so that you may charge certain persons not to teach any different doctrine, nor to devote themselves to myths and endless genealogies, which promote speculations rather than the stewardship from God that is by faith" (1 Tim. 1:3–4).

- "Have nothing to do with irreverent, silly myths. Rather train yourself for godliness" (1 Tim. 4:7).
- "He has an unhealthy craving for controversy and for quarrels about words, which produce envy, dissension, slander, evil suspicions, and constant friction" (1 Tim. 6:4–5).
- "O Timothy, guard the deposit entrusted to you. Avoid the irreverent babble and contradictions of what is falsely called 'knowledge,' for by professing it some have swerved from the faith" (1 Tim. 6:20–21).
- "Remind them of these things, and charge them before God not to quarrel about words, which does no good, but only ruins the hearers" (2 Tim. 2:14).
- "But avoid irreverent babble, for it will lead people into more and more ungodliness" (2 Tim. 2:16).
- "Have nothing to do with foolish, ignorant controversies; you know that they breed quarrels" (2 Tim. 2:23).
- "For the time is coming when people will not endure sound teaching, but having itching ears they will accumulate for themselves teachers to suit their own passions, and will turn away from listening to the truth and wander off into myths" (2 Tim. 4:3–4).
- "Rebuke them sharply, that they may be sound in the faith, not devoting themselves to Jewish myths and the commands of people who turn away from the truth" (Titus 1:13–14).
- "But avoid foolish controversies, genealogies, dissensions, and quarrels about the law, for they are unprofitable and worthless" (Titus 3:9).

Paul never tells us the exact nature of the false teaching Timothy is facing in Ephesus, or Titus is facing in Crete. In both cases it seems to involve certain myths and genealogies, it seems to be highly speculative and vain (he calls these views "silly" and "irreverent"), and it seems to breed quarreling and dissensions. Repeatedly, Paul commands that Titus and Timothy steer clear of these controversies because they do not produce godliness.

Now, we don't face the same threats that Timothy and Titus faced. But surely we have all witnessed (or been a part of) theological debates that do not advance the godliness of those involved but instead promote quarreling and vain speculation. We should constantly remind ourselves of Paul's prioritization of the gospel and his pastoral burden for godliness in these passages. The goal of our theology is "a pure heart and a good conscience and a sincere faith" (1 Tim. 1:5); theological debate that is disconnected from this goal must be avoided. As Kevin DeYoung put it, drawing attention to these same passages, "We should steer clear of theological wrangling that is speculative (goes beyond Scripture), vain (more about being right than being helpful), endless (no real answer is possible or desired), and needless (mere semantics)."[21]

One of the ways theological wrangling harms the holiness of the church is by discouraging love among Christians. In his classic book *The Cure for Church Divisions*, Richard Baxter cautions us, "They are dangerously mistaken that think that Satan has but one way to men's damnation. There are as many ways to hell, as there be to the extinguishing of love."[22] Baxter goes on to suggest that an overly strict and fault-finding spirit is one of Satan's principal means to discourage love among Christians:

---

21. Kevin DeYoung, "Where and How Do We Draw the Line?," *Tabletalk* 36, no. 7 (July 2012): 14.

22. Richard Baxter, *The Cure for Church Divisions, or, Directions for Weak Christians to Keep Them from Being Dividers or Troublers of the Church with Some Directions to the Pastors How to Deal with Such Christians* (London: Symmons, 1670), 1.2.6, spelling and capitalization updated.

> Satan will pretend to any sort of strictness, by which he can mortify love. If you can devise any such strictness of opinions, or exactness in church orders, or strictness in worship, as will but help to kill men's love, and set the churches in divisions, Satan will be your helper, and will be the strictest and exactest of you all: He will reprove Christ as a Sabbath breaker, and as a gluttonous person, and a wine-bibber, and a friend (or companion) of publicans and sinners, and as an enemy to Caesar too.[23]

As a result, Baxter warns that a harsh, critical spirit associates us with Satan:

> You think when a wrathful envious heat is kindled in you against men for their fault, that it is certainly a zeal of God's exciting: But mark whether it have not more wrath than love in it: and whether it tend not more to disgrace your brother than to cure him, or to make parties and divisions, than to heal them: if it be so, if St. James be not deceived, you are deceived as to the author of your zeal (James 3:15–16) and it has a worse original than you suspect.[24]

It might sound harsh to say that a loveless, exacting spirit comes from the devil. Yet the Scripture gives us ground to see that sinful behavior plays into the hands of Satan. Opponents of the gospel have been "captured by [the devil] to do his will" (2 Tim. 2:26). Satan is "at work in the sons of disobedience" (Eph. 2:2). Even among Christians, sin gives him "opportunity" (Eph. 4:27).

Jesus even calls Peter—the rock of the church—"Satan" for his worldly wisdom (Matt. 16:23). Anyone who has witnessed firsthand the destructive consequences of loveless zeal in the

---

23. Baxter, *Cure for Church Divisions*, 1.2.6.
24. Baxter, *Cure for Church Divisions*, 1.2.6.

church will understand how such a spirit can serve Satan's purposes. Christians are well capable of "devouring" one another (Gal. 5:15).

Baxter's words remind us that theological zeal must be subjected to the test of love. Not all zeal is from God. Even when the error we oppose is a deadly heresy, our aim must be to heal, not to disgrace. And in all our theological engagements with each other, we must be sure that our ultimate goal is to promote the godliness and welfare of the church.

Finding Our Identity in the Gospel

Unnecessary division is often a heart issue. It is easy for a spirit of self-justification to ride shotgun with our secondary distinctives. Much doctrinal separatism stems from finding our identity in our theological distinctives when we should be finding it in the gospel. As John Newton wisely warned, "Self-righteousness can feed upon doctrines, as well as works!"[25] John Calvin went so far as to claim that "pride or haughtiness is the cause and commencement of all contentions."[26]

We know there is a spirit of self-justification about our theology when we feel superior to Christians from other tribes and groups, or when a particular believer, church, or group unduly annoys us. It is one thing to disagree with another Christian. That is inevitable to anyone who thinks. It is another thing when our disagreement takes an attitude of contempt, condescension, or undue suspicion toward those with whom we disagree. If our identity is riding on our differences with other believers, we will tend to major in the study of differences. We may even find ourselves *looking* for faults in others in order to define ourselves.

25. John Newton, "On Controversy," in *The Works of John Newton*, vol. 1 (New Haven, CT: Nathan Whiting, 1824), 160.

26. John Calvin, *1 and 2 Corinthians*, trans. William Pringle, vol. 20 of *Calvin's Commentaries* (Grand Rapids, MI: Baker, 1989), 158.

When we notice the unhealthy symptoms of doctrinal sectarianism in our hearts, we need to return our deepest level of emotional loyalty to Jesus himself. He is the one who died for us. He is the one to whom we will ultimately answer, and his business is what we are about in the first place. Jesus alone is worthy of our ultimate commitment, and all other doctrines find their proper place in relation to him. As we return to Christ himself for our deepest placement and identity, he will help us hold our convictions with both confidence and grace.

2

The Danger of Doctrinal Minimalism

Doctrinal separatism is a real problem. But it is not the only one. In fact, we often react to this problem by swinging to the complete opposite end of the spectrum. Martin Luther compared human reason to a drunken man on horseback, who, when propped up on one side, will tumble over the other. So it is with our theological posture and the difficulty of finding the wisdom of *poise*. As Richard Baxter observed, "Many an error is taken up by going too far from other men's faults."[1]

The overall trajectory of our culture, particularly among younger generations, probably tends more toward doctrinal minimalism and indifferentism. Four hundred years ago, if you took a different view on baptism, you may have gotten drowned for it. Today we rightly recoil at that, but I worry that we sometimes swing to the opposite extreme. This is the mind-set that says: "Let's stop dividing over doctrine! It just

1. Quoted in Iain H. Murray, *Evangelicalism Divided: A Record of the Crucial Change in the Years 1950 to 2000* (Carlisle, PA: Banner of Truth, 2000), 299.

hurts people. Let's just love Jesus and feed the poor." This is doctrinal minimalism.

As much as we may appreciate the intention, carrying out this statement is not so simple. For instance, to "stop dividing and just love Jesus," we must define "Jesus." When we do that, doctrinal division is unavoidable. In fact, we actually benefit from divisions that have already taken place and, in many cases, have not been resolved. To pick just one example, it took the early church generations of dispute and division to work out (among other related points) that Jesus has two distinct natures; he is not a divine-human hybrid. If we affirm with the Chalcedonian definition of 451—which most Christians acknowledge as ecumenical—that Jesus is "to be acknowledged in two natures, inconfusedly, unchangeably, indivisibly, inseparably," then we are dividing from the monophysites of the early church and many Oriental Orthodox Christians today.[2] This is just one example of how doctrinal division is inherent in using the name Jesus. And there are many more examples we could use.

Ultimately, doctrinal division cannot be avoided. Believe anything, and you are disbelieving its opposite and therefore dividing, in some sense, from those who don't share your belief.

Do Nonessential Doctrines Matter?

But many of us today have seen such destructive tendencies related to doctrinal disagreement that we want to stay as far away as possible. Sometimes we want to avoid talking about doctrine completely (though this is ultimately impossible). Another tendency is to reduce our doctrinal focus to a small body of truths related to the gospel message and then ignore everything else. I have often heard people say, "It's not a gospel issue; it's just

2. Monophysitism is simply the view that Jesus has one nature. To be clear, most Oriental Orthodox Christians today, though rejecting Chalcedonian Christology, do not affirm monophysitism but rather hold a more nuanced view labeled miaphysitism.

a secondary issue." And, of course, we should distinguish between the gospel and secondary issues. But if we stop at this basic distinction, we risk obscuring the significance of secondary doctrines. I worry that when people make this distinction, they mean something like "It's a secondary issue; *therefore, it doesn't really matter*."

While I sympathize with the instinct to focus on the gospel, we must recognize that distinguishing between the gospel and other doctrines is a complicated task. For example, doctrines can be "secondary" or "nonessential" to the gospel and yet still make a difference in *how we uphold* the gospel. Consider the well-known saying, often falsely attributed to Augustine but actually dating from the early seventeenth century: "In essentials, unity; in nonessentials, liberty; and in all things, charity." So far as it goes, this assertion has much to commend it. A weakness, however, is that it is working with only two categories: essential and nonessential. Let's go back to our fourfold schema:

- First-rank doctrines are *essential* to the gospel.
- Second-rank doctrines are *urgent* for the church (but not essential to the gospel).
- Third-rank doctrines are *important* to Christian theology (but not essential to the gospel or necessarily urgent for the church).
- Fourth-rank doctrines are *indifferent* (they are theologically unimportant).

I use the term "important" for the third category deliberately, though I realize it could be misleading. It reflects the concern of this chapter that *many doctrines are significant even if we don't divide over them*. "Important" is, of course, a relative term—hopefully, placing it after "urgent" and "essential" will make it clear that I do not mean "important for salvation" or even "important for productive collaboration." But again—to press the point—the fact that a particular doctrine is not important for salvation or partnership does not mean that it cannot be important in *any* sense.

Why is this so? Why not equate "nonessential" with "indifferent," and lump together everything in categories 2–4? Here I'll give four brief reasons for the significance of nonessential doctrines, though there might be more.

1. Nonessential Doctrines Are Significant to Scripture

Imagine getting a letter from your long-lost love. Every sentence is precious to you. You wouldn't shrug at anything. So also, if we regard the Bible as divinely inspired, we should reverence all its contents. It's the very word of God to us. It is holy, from above. Every sentence should be treasured.

One consequence of downplaying the importance of nonessential doctrines is, however inadvertently, downplaying Scripture itself. At the start of a book on church government, the nineteenth-century Scottish theologian Thomas Witherow observed,

> It is very common for professing Christians to draw a distinction between *essentials* and *non-essentials* in religion, and to infer that if any fact or doctrine rightly belongs to the latter class it must be a matter of very little importance, and may in practice be safely set at naught.[3]

Witherow acknowledged the validity of the distinction between essential and nonessential doctrines but objected to the common inference that some parts of the Bible don't matter. When-

3. Thomas Witherow, *Which Is the Apostolic Church? An Inquiry at the Oracles of God as to Whether Any Existing Form of Church Government Is of Divine Right*, ed. R. M. Patterson (Philadelphia: Presbyterian Board of Publication, 1851), 5, his emphasis.

ever we ask whether something is essential, we must also ask, "Essential for what?" Everything God reveals in Scripture is essential for something, or it wouldn't be there. "Nonessential for salvation" does not mean of no importance at all.

> To say that, because a fact of divine revelation is not essential to salvation, it must of necessity be unimportant, and may or may not be received by us, is to assert a principle, the application of which would make havoc of our Christianity. For, what are the truths essential to salvation? Are they not these: That there is a God; that all men are sinners; that the Son of God died upon the cross to make atonement for the guilty; and that whosoever believes on the Lord Jesus Christ will be saved? . . . But if all the other truths of revelation are unimportant, because they happen to be non-essentials, it follows that the Word of God itself is in the main unimportant; for by far the greatest portion of it is occupied with matters the knowledge of which . . . is not absolutely indispensable to the everlasting happiness of men.[4]

Witherow's concern is particularly understandable in light of the sheer amount of the Bible devoted to what ultimately must be categorized as nonessential doctrines. Whatever else we say about the Bible, we can say with certainty that it is not a bare-bones, minimalistic document. It is amazingly *detailed*. Consider the fine-tuned instruction for all the different parts of the tabernacle (Ex. 25–30), or the number of Proverbs devoted to mundane topics like talking loudly early in the morning (Prov. 27:14), or the length and finesse of Paul's teaching on marriage and singleness (1 Cor. 7). God apparently thought it important for us to have this information. If we isolate everything outside

4. Witherow, *Which Is the Apostolic Church?*, 6–7.

the gospel as a matter of indifference, we end up trivializing the majority of what God has communicated to us.

The Bible itself commends an attitude of eager responsiveness to God's word in its entirety. Confusion may be an understandable response to some passages, and grief to others; but indifference should never be our response. Thus the Berean Jews are described as "more noble" than the Thessalonians because they received Paul's preaching "with all eagerness, examining the Scriptures daily to see if these things were so" (Acts 17:11). One thinks of King Josiah tearing his clothes when the law is rediscovered (2 Kings 22:11), or God's commendation of the one who

> is humble and contrite in spirit
> and trembles at [God's] word. (Isa. 66:2)

A casual, take-it-or-leave-it attitude about theology is totally incompatible with how we are to receive the word of God. Its contents may call for trembling and tearing of clothes, but never shrugging.

In his classic book *Knowing God*, J. I. Packer even suggests that a love for all of God's truth is a distinguishing mark of regeneration. After quoting from the psalmist's love of God's law in Psalm 119, Packer writes: "Do not all children of God long, with the psalmist, to know just as much about our heavenly Father as we can learn? Is not, indeed, the fact that we have received a love for his truth in this way one proof that we shall have been born again?"[5] Every regenerate believer should be characterized by the claim of Psalm 1:2:

> His delight is in the law of the LORD,
> and on his law he meditates day and night.

5. J. I. Packer, *Knowing God* (Downers Grove, IL: InterVarsity Press, 1973), 22.

Therefore, even if we ultimately conclude that the interpretation of a particular passage is not worth our dividing from other Christians, it doesn't follow that we should relegate that passage to the realm of *adiaphora* and say, "Who cares?" Rather, our love for the Lord who breathed it to us—and our reverence for it as his breathed word—should compel diligent study and effort to understand it as much as we can, as the Bereans did.

2. Nonessential Doctrines Are Significant to Church History

When we visit a memorial or museum devoted to a historical event, we rightly pay respect to the sacrifices others have made. The Normandy American Cemetery and Memorial reminds us of the cost of our current freedoms. The Holocaust Museum in Washington, DC, sobers us with a reminder of the atrocities we are capable of as human beings. We do well to recognize and to show respect for the suffering and sacrifice of those who came before us.

The sacrifices Christians have made throughout church history can and should play an analogous role for us. Historically, Christians have been willing to shed their blood not only for the basic gospel message but also for a body of doctrinal truths they have understood as important to the gospel. Consider those who gave their lives in protest of abuses within the church before and after the Reformation. Jan Hus was burned at the stake for a number of issues, including his speaking out against indulgences and papal power. After refusing a final opportunity to recant, he prayed out: "Lord Jesus, it is for thee that I patiently endure this cruel death. I pray thee to have mercy on my enemies."[6] William Tyndale was executed in no small part for his writing against Henry VIII's annulment of his

6. Justo L. González, *The Story of Christianity*, vol. 1, *The Early Church to the Dawn of the Reformation* (New York: HarperCollins, 1984), 351.

marriage to Catherine of Aragon. The Anglican bishops Hugh Latimer, Nicholas Ridley, and Thomas Cranmer were willing to be burned at the stake for their opposition to Roman Catholic doctrines like the Mass and the papacy. It is reported that when his sentence was given, Latimer said, "I thank God most heartily that He hath prolonged my life to this end, that I may in this case glorify God by that kind of death."[7]

This side of the ecumenical movement, the mood in Catholic-Protestant relations is very different. Secularism is a quickly rising tide. Many voices are calling for an end to the Reformation.[8] And, indeed, there have been important doctrinal developments in Protestant-Catholic dialogue. In my view, we should welcome efforts of dialogue and rapprochement amid the various divisions of Christendom and appreciate much of what is already happening. At the same time, we should not exaggerate what has been accomplished. Important differences remain.

Whatever our approach to the complex challenge of ecumenical effort today, we must not ignore or downplay the issues that remain on the table. To identify certain issues as unresolved is not itself divisive. J. Gresham Machen explains, "It is often said that the divided state of Christendom is an evil, and so it is. But the evil consists in the existence of the errors which cause the divisions and not at all in the recognition of those errors when once they exist."[9] The cause of true ecumenism is not served by a nonchalant posture toward theology that trivializes or bypasses the issues that have caused separation in the first place.

7. John McClintock and James Stock, *Cyclopaedia of Biblical, Theological, and Ecclesiastical Literature*, vol. 5 (New York: Harper and Brothers, 1891), 261.

8. E.g., Mark A. Noll and Carolyn Nystrom, *Is the Reformation Over? An Evangelical Assessment of Contemporary Roman Catholicism* (Grand Rapids, MI: Baker Academic, 2005).

9. J. Gresham Machen, *Christianity and Liberalism* (New York: Macmillan, 1923), 50.

Bearing in mind the sacrifices of the past helps us remember that. It is difficult to countenance the charred flesh of Latimer and Ridley, for instance, and then remain indifferent to the disputes about the Lord's Supper that led to their circumstance. Of course, we may not always agree with exactly how Christians of previous eras have taken a stand. But we need not consider them infallible in order to appreciate and learn from their example. We can and should be sobered by the courage, carefulness, and conviction with which our predecessors in the faith pursued theological integrity, even on various nonessential doctrines.

3. Nonessential Doctrines Are Significant to the Christian Life

I don't regard my understanding of divine sovereignty, for instance, as a "gospel issue" in all its nuance, and I gladly welcome as brothers and sisters in Christ those who hold to an Arminian/Wesleyan view (and I have much to learn from them). At the same time, my understanding of God's sovereignty has significant implications for everyday, practical Christianity. For example, it affects my prayer life in various ways. So it would be a mistake, and disrespectful to both Calvinists and Arminians, to shrug off this issue as a matter of irrelevance.

We should remember that we are often not fully aware of the role our theology is designed to play. Consider the doctrine of Christ's heavenly intercession. While I'm convinced this doctrine is part of the gospel, we are not always conscious of it in our engagement with the gospel. One can conceivably understand and receive the gospel without knowing much about Christ's intercession. (I was a Christian for many years before I knew what it meant.) At the same time, I agree with William Symington that Christ's intercession is one of the most nourishing, edifying doctrines in the entire realm of Christian belief.[10] What a tragedy to brush aside this doctrine simply because it is not essential to receiving the gospel! We cannot always chart on a graph how our view of Christ's intercession will affect our relationship with him on any given day. It is perilous to dismiss a doctrine as pointless simply because it might not qualify as a first-rank point of theology.

Consider, as another example, the nature of Christ's presence in the Lord's Supper. I personally hold a broadly Calvinist/ Reformed understanding in which Christ is really present in the elements, but in a spiritual manner. However, I would not have a problem serving on staff at a church with someone who holds to, say, a Zwinglian memorialist view of the Lord's Supper, in which we remember Christ's sacrifice but do not feast upon it as a means of grace. I do not divide from others over this issue.

But this does not mean that the differences between these two views count for nothing. They have significant pastoral and personal repercussions for how we lead and partake of the Lord's Supper. And they tie into larger disputes that have been going on throughout the history of the church, most significantly the Protestant concern of idolatry in the Catholic understanding of the Mass.[11]

There is a sad poverty of awareness in simply bypassing all this historical discussion and adopting an up-for-grabs mentality in which theology functions like the people in the book of Judges, when "everyone did what was right in his own eyes" (Judg. 21:25).

In his classic polemic against liberal theology, *Christianity and Liberalism*, J. Gresham Machen devotes the first chapter

10. William Symington, *On the Atonement and Intercession of Jesus Christ* (Pittsburgh, PA: United Presbyterian Board of Publication, 1864), iv.

11. The other major views are transubstantiation (the Roman Catholic view in which the elements of bread and wine become the body and blood of Christ) and consubstantiation (the Lutheran view that the body and blood of Christ are "in, with, and under" the elements).

to defending the claim that doctrine is essential to orthodox Christianity. At one point, he pauses to clarify that "we do not mean, insisting upon the doctrinal basis of Christianity, that all points of doctrine are equally important. It is perfectly possible for Christian fellowship to be maintained despite differences of opinion."[12] He then identifies five examples of doctrines Christians may disagree on: (1) the nature of the millennium, (2) the mode and efficacy of the sacraments, (3) the nature and prerogatives of Christian ministry (here he has in mind the Anglican doctrine of apostolic succession, in particular), (4) Calvinism versus Arminianism, and (5) differences between the church of Rome and evangelical Protestantism (though he describes this final example as "more serious").

The way Machen expounds each of these points is a good example of theological triage. In each case, he looks for where unity can be maintained without diluting the importance of the issue. For example, in the context of his exposition of the second of these five points, the mode and efficacy of the sacraments, Machen acknowledges that this topic "is indeed serious, and to deny its seriousness is a far greater controversy than to take the wrong side in the controversy itself."[13] Machen laments the division between Luther and Zwingli on this point in Marburg in 1529, which prevented the union of Lutheran and Reformed branches of Protestantism. He emphasizes the tragedy of this dispute, faulting Luther, but cautions us against belittling the importance of the issues at stake:

> Luther was wrong about the Supper, but not nearly so wrong as he would have been if, being wrong, he had said to his opponents: "Brethren, this matter is a trifle; and it makes really very little difference what a man thinks about

12. Machen, *Christianity and Liberalism*, 48.
13. Machen, *Christianity and Liberalism*, 50.

> the table of the Lord." Such indifferentism would have been far more deadly than all the divisions between the branches of the Church. A Luther who would have compromised with regard to the Lord's Supper never would have said at the Diet of Worms, "Here I stand, I cannot do otherwise, God help me, Amen." Indifferentism about doctrine makes no heroes of the faith.[14]

On many other issues, as well, we might say with Machen: better to be wrong than indifferent.

4. Nonessential Doctrines Are Significant to Essential Doctrines

In a Roman Catholic context, Edward T. Oakes argues for a "hierarchy" of doctrine, reasoning that the lesser issues gain their importance in relation to the greater ones:

> The church has long recognized that she speaks with different levels of authority and addresses issues of greater and lesser moment. Indeed the very truths she seeks both to propound and to defend are themselves arranged according to a certain hierarchy, with some doctrines of greater significance (among which would of course include Christology) and others not so much of lesser significance but ones that *gain their force*, so to speak, by their relation to the truths of greater moment. Of course, truths that are implications of "higher" truths are not *less* true; rather, they gain their truth-value from their relation (as implications) to more fundamental doctrines.[15]

14. Machen, *Christianity and Liberalism*, 50–51.

15. Edward T. Oakes, *Infinity Dwindled to Infancy: A Catholic and Evangelical Christology* (Grand Rapids, MI: Eerdmans, 2011), 395, his emphasis. I was directed to this quotation by Luke Stamps, "Let's Get Our Theological Priorities Straight," The Gospel Coalition, June 4, 2012, https://www.thegospelcoalition.org/article/lets-get-our-theological-priorities-straight/. As Stamps notes, "One need not embrace Oakes's understanding of the Roman Catholic Magisterium in order to appreciate his point."

If lesser and greater truths have a relation to each other, then it is dangerous to assume that so long as a doctrine is not part of the gospel, it is of no importance to the gospel. Many second- and third-rank doctrines will influence *how* we experience and/or uphold the gospel. B. B. Warfield reflected this instinct when he wrote: "Why make much of minor points of difference between those who serve the one Christ? Because a pure gospel is worth preserving."[16]

How do doctrines that are not themselves the gospel help us preserve a *pure* gospel?

Some doctrines *picture* the gospel. For instance, Paul teaches that there is a profound connection between the marriage relationship and Christ's relationship with the church (Eph. 5:32). That is why the way the church has historically approached the interpretation of the Song of Solomon is not a crazy instinct. It is also one reason why it is so problematic when Christians acquiesce to changing definitions of marriage today.

Some doctrines *protect* the gospel. For instance, it is possible to have a powerful grasp of the gospel and yet a relatively low view of Scripture. In my mind, C. S. Lewis would fit this category, though we'd have to flesh out what we mean by "low"—his view was not as low as it could be! At the same time, it would be foolish to conclude that what we believe about Scripture has no bearing on the quality of our witness to the gospel. Far from it! Upholding a high view of God's word will reverberate into practically every way we seek to fulfill our calling as the people of God.

Some doctrines *pertain* to the gospel. Rare is a doctrine that can be hermetically sealed off from the rest of the Christian faith. Thus, downplaying secondary doctrines can leave

16. Benjamin B. Warfield, *Selected Shorter Writings*, vol. 2 (Nutley, NJ: Presbyterian and Reformed, 1973), 665–66.

the primary ones blander, quieter, and more vulnerable. Take, for instance, your view of the relationship between Scripture and tradition. It is not easy to say how this issue constitutes or materially contributes to the gospel. But, of course, it is a significant point of difference among different Christian traditions that has all kinds of consequences in how our theology plays out. Those who are aware of how differences on this issue have played out in church history cannot regard it as a matter of indifference.

There Is a Time to Fight over Doctrine

Most of us recognize that a pugnacious, mean-spirited attitude toward theological controversy is antithetical to the gospel. But we must also say that so is an *unwillingness* to fight over doctrine. Doctrinal minimalism and doctrinal indifferentism have no backbone. A doctrinal minimalist is unlikely to say, with Paul, "Let God be true though every one were a liar" (Rom. 3:4); the indifferent are unlikely to be so committed to the gospel as to anathematize angels that depart from it (Gal. 1:8).

Each member of the Westminster Assembly who fought for the reformation of the Church of England in the mid-seventeenth century was required to take a vow upon admittance to the assembly:

> I do seriously promise and vow, in the presence of Almighty God, that in this Assembly, whereof I am a member, I will maintain nothing in point of doctrine, but what I believe to be most agreeable to the word of God; nor in point of discipline, but what may make most for God's glory; and the peace and good of this church.[17]

17. *The Westminster Confession of Faith* (Glasgow: Free Presbyterian, 1966), 13.

Modern approaches to theology are often too casual to have a place for vow-taking like this. We can learn a lot from these divines about the sacredness of our task.

Theology is done *coram Deo* (before the face of God). The glory of God and the good of the church are at stake. Nothing but our deepest sincerity and diligence is sufficient for this undertaking. It will take all the courage we have.

3

My Journey on Secondary and Tertiary Doctrines

It is generally safe to locate yourself between two extremes. That is essentially what I have done in the last two chapters. Hopefully, this has been helpful as an orienting starting point, especially because, as I have said, many of us tend in one direction or the other. But now comes the more difficult work of probing where between these two extremes the path of wisdom lies.

As an entry point, I want to share my story with you. My interest in theological triage is not academic. It is very personal and has affected my life profoundly. I never set out looking to divide over doctrine. I was simply minding my own business, reading theology books. That there might be *consequences* from my reading was an afterthought. But it also became unavoidable.

Let me start at the beginning.

I was baptized as an infant in the Church of Scotland (which is Presbyterian). I grew up attending primarily Presbyterian churches (Presbyterian Church in America), as well as an Evangelical Free church for a few years as a child. During college I worked with the youth groups of two different Presbyterian churches, and after college I went to a Presbyterian seminary (Covenant Theological Seminary, in St. Louis).

There is no way I can sufficiently emphasize my gratitude for my experiences in these contexts. The various churches I attended while growing up I remember as healthy and happy places. I became a Christian at one of them, Crosslife Evangelical Free Church in Libertyville, Illinois. I am increasingly aware of how rare it is to be able to look back at your childhood experiences in church and not have baggage, so I'm grateful.

Just before I started high school, my family moved to Georgia, where my dad pastored First Presbyterian Church in Augusta. I got deeply involved in this church's youth group, and I will always be grateful for the influence it had on me. My mind is saturated with happy memories from mission trips, beach days, times of worship, and so forth. I also attended a Christian school for the first time in my life, and the friendships and experiences I had there had a huge effect upon me. This was a profoundly formative time in my life spiritually, and some of the happiest memories and deepest friendships in my life come from those years.

During college I went back to work with my youth group for several summers, and during one summer worked with the youth group at another church as well. It was during this time that I felt a call to ministry. I had been struggling (without fully realizing it) with a hesitation that since others in my family had been in ministry, it would not be genuine of me to follow that same path. But that summer, as I taught the Bible and led worship with my guitar and pursued students with the gospel,

I found myself thinking, "This is why I'm on the planet. This is what I want to do with the rest of my life."

I realized that while my family was not a reason to go into ministry, it was also not a reason *not* to go into ministry. This freed me to simply consider what Jesus was calling *me* to do. I will always owe a debt to First Presbyterian Church, not only for the spiritually formative role it played in my life during my high school years but also for giving me opportunities during my college years that started me on the vocational path I am now walking.

After college my wife and I attended Covenant Seminary, where I pursued a theology degree and she got a counseling degree. Covenant gave us a beautiful portrait of what "gospel-centeredness" is at its best. In fact, our years there were so formative that we often speak of establishing a "Covenant Seminary ethos" as the whole goal of our ministry, wherever we go. It's difficult to describe exactly what a "Covenant Seminary ethos" is, but it has to do with a combination of theological depth and relational warmth. Most of the other contexts I've been in tend to emphasize *either* the theology *or* the gentleness. We sensed something healthy and beautiful about the theological culture at Covenant, and we have always felt discontent with pursuing anything less.

Sometime during my years at Covenant I also started listening to sermons by Tim Keller, a Presbyterian pastor. I cannot describe the formative influence his sermons (and now books) have had on me. When I am facing a ministry or theological issue, it's rare that I *don't* say, "I wonder what Tim Keller thinks about that?" I'm hugely indebted to his ministry.

My point in saying all this is that there was no personal dissatisfaction, in any way, that drove me to look for a denominational change. Instead, I look back upon my time within Presbyterianism with gratitude and nostalgia.

Immersed in a Study of Baptism

But a problem came as I studied the issue of baptism. During my final semester of college at the University of Georgia, I began reading everything I could on baptism. I had never really bothered to study it before, but now that I was heading into the pastorate, I knew I had to face it because it would affect where I could be ordained. To be ordained in a Presbyterian context, you have to subscribe to the Westminster Standards, which affirm that the children of one or more believing parents should be baptized as infants.[1]

I continued to wrestle with this topic upon arriving at Covenant. During my first year there, I made this issue my personal project. I remember conversations about baptism with friends that lasted well into the night. I remember office hours with professors on this topic and engaging discussions in class. I remember one long afternoon that fall struggling with Pierre-Charles Marcel's *The Biblical Doctrine of Infant Baptism*, and another whole day that winter occupied with Paul Jewett's *Infant Baptism and the Covenant of Grace*. And lots of other books like these, on both sides of the issue.

By April of that year, my convictions had solidified against paedobaptism (this is another term for infant baptism) and in favor of credobaptism (the view that the proper subjects of baptism are those who make a credible profession of faith). My wife and I joined a Baptist church and I was baptized (dunked in a river, to be exact). This book is not the place to get into the reasons why I made this change, which I've written about elsewhere. Here I don't want to annoy my paedobaptist readers any more than necessary.

1. The Westminster Standards are the documents drawn up by the Westminster Assembly in the mid-seventeenth century, especially the Westminster Confession of Faith, the Westminster Shorter Catechism, and the Westminster Larger Catechism. Many Reformed and Presbyterian traditions look to these documents as doctrinal standards.

Now that I was unable to be ordained in Presbyterian circles, I faced a challenge. All my networking was in the circles I grew up in, so I didn't know exactly where I would fit in within the world of credobaptists. I ended up doing a pastoral internship at a Baptist church, where I got to study issues of church polity more closely. This was, yet again, a positive experience. We were blessed to observe a healthy and fruitful church up close (Capitol Hill Baptist Church in Washington, DC).

But around this time I began to struggle with mainstream Baptist practices concerning baptism. The traditional Baptist view is that baptism following a credible profession of faith is not only the biblically prescribed practice but also a precondition for church membership and participation in the Lord's Supper. For instance, the 2000 Baptist Faith and Message, the statement of faith for the Southern Baptist Convention (the largest Baptist denomination in the world), stipulates concerning baptism, "Being a church ordinance, it is prerequisite to the privileges of church membership and to the Lord's Supper."[2] This practice, particularly the restriction of the Lord's Supper, is sometimes referred to as the position of "strict Baptists."

A related issue is the proper mode of baptism. Historically, Baptists have typically held that baptism must be by immersion. For instance, the Second London Baptist Confession of Faith of 1689 stipulates, "Immersion—the dipping of the person in water—is necessary for the due administration of this ordinance."[3] People today often conflate these two issues—the proper *subjects* of baptism and the proper *mode* of baptism. We should remember that the *who* and *how* questions are distinguishable, though they often go together.

2. 2000 Baptist Faith and Message, 7. For a well-argued expression of this view, see Bobby Jamieson, *Going Public: Why Baptism Is Required for Church Membership* (Nashville: B&H, 2015).

3. The Second London Baptist Confession of Faith of 1689, 29.4.

Now, different Baptist traditions and individuals differ on these issues. It's complicated. Some Baptist churches today require baptism for membership but not for the Lord's Supper, for instance. Similarly, many Baptist churches are softer on the issue of mode—they might say, for instance, that immersion is the proper mode but that sprinkling or pouring, while not preferable, still constitutes baptism (especially in special circumstances, like water scarcity or health difficulties). Historically, even prominent Baptists have differed on these issues. John Bunyan, for example, the author of the famous book *The Pilgrim's Progress*, allowed paedobaptists to join his church. In his 1673 *Differences about Water Baptism No Bar to Communion*, he offered ten reasons to support this practice.

I've wrestled with these issues, and I've grown to appreciate their complexity while ultimately finding myself unable to affirm the stricter Baptist practices. This has left me in a somewhat lonely and isolated place denominationally, since it entails that I am unacceptable for ordination among both Presbyterians and many Baptists. It has led to several closed doors since that time as well.

From End Times to the Creation Days

Having left the world of Presbyterianism, I was navigating the broader world of evangelicalism. These were unfamiliar and choppy waters. Suddenly my amillennialism was becoming conspicuous.

Amillennialism is the view that the "thousand years" of Revelation 20:4–10 refers to the spiritual reign of Christ from heaven during the church age. The alternative views are premillennialism, which holds that the second coming of Christ will come before the millennium, and postmillennialism, which holds that that second coming of Christ will follow a millennium. Most evangelical churches in the United States trend toward premillennialism, particularly *dispensational* premillennialism, which emphasizes the literal thousand-year reign of Christ from Jerusalem and fulfillment of Old Testament prophecy concerning ethnic Israel during this time.[4] In my experience, a lot of Christians are not even aware that there are other views than this.

Being amillennial had never been a problem back in my little Presbyterian harbor. I naively thought other harbors might be equally accommodating. After all, as I will discuss in chapter 6, premillennialism was virtually absent from the church between Augustine and the seventeenth century, and it really only began in its current form in the nineteen century.

I was surprised to discover how many denominations and individual churches still require premillennialism in their statements of faith. Thus, having effectively isolated myself from the majority of Christendom over baptism, I realized I had now further distanced myself from a vast number of the remaining free and nondenominational churches over the millennium. This separation was in no way my intention or desire. It simply resulted from studying the issues.

Next came my ordination paper. I had landed on the staff of a nondenominational Congregational church, and part of my ordination process involved writing out a lengthy personal statement of faith. In the section on eschatology (the doctrine of the last things, or end times), I mentioned in one brief sentence partial preterism, an eschatological view that holds that some biblical prophecies about the end times were fulfilled in the first century.

4. For instance, a 2011 poll conducted by the National Association of Evangelicals found that among evangelicals, "65 percent identify with premillennial theology, 13 percent with amillennial and 4 percent with postmillennial. Seventeen percent responded 'other'" ("Premillennialism Reigns in Evangelical Theology," National Association of Evangelicals, January 2011, https://www.nae.net/premillennialism-reigns-in-evangelical-theology.

Somehow, either through a mistake or unfamiliarity with the terms, it got around to a few other church members that I was simply a preterist. If you know this discussion at all, you know that preterism and partial preterism are very different. Partial preterism says that *some* eschatological events are already fulfilled (like the so-called great tribulation). Full preterism says that *everything* is already fulfilled (we are currently living in the new heavens and new earth, Jesus has already returned, and so on).

Needless to say, it is important to distinguish between these two vastly different positions. In fact, I'd say the difference is that of orthodoxy versus heresy. I don't use the *h* word lightly, but I use it for full preterism. Partial preterism, on the other hand, is a relatively modest view held by conservative evangelical theologians like the late R. C. Sproul, though it's largely absent from the broader evangelical consciousness.

So, as you can imagine, I had some interesting conversations with church members who just heard the term "preterist" and didn't know what to make of it. Thankfully, the pastors presiding over this process were gracious enough to approve my ordination despite their own disagreements with my view.[5]

Ultimately, I was ordained in the CCCC (Conservative Congregational Christian Conference), which is a smaller denomination of Congregational churches. CCCC has been a good fit for me theologically, since it emphasizes unity in essentials and liberty in nonessentials. The conference has clear position papers on social issues like marriage and abortion but is relatively open on various doctrinal issues like women in ministry, spiritual gifts, the millennium, and so forth.

---

5. To be clear, I don't exactly like calling myself a "partial preterist" because the terminology is confusing, and because I put more emphasis than many other partial preterists on complexities of prophetic fulfillment that I think we see in the Old Testament, like telescoping, dual fulfillment, intervening historical contingencies, etc. But I own that I'm broadly in this camp.

I have also appreciated being a part of a specific, recognizable, Protestant denomination whose roots can be traced back through church history. Congregationalism has a rich heritage in our country, embracing figures from Jonathan Edwards to Harold John Ockenga, and playing a key role in the founding of institutions from Harvard University to the National Association of Evangelicals. In Puritan New England, much of Protestant Christianity was Congregational, and its history in our country is an outgrowth of the Puritan struggle in the Church of England, specifically among "independents" like John Owen who contributed to the Savoy Declaration. Moreover, from the beginning, Congregationalism positioned itself as part of the historic church, as did the other major branches of Protestantism, contra many Anabaptists. So Congregationalism is one way of placing yourself in the larger stream of church history. It is one of the little rivulets in the river of orthodox Christianity. I'm grateful to have found a denominational "home," at least in terms of my ordination.[6]

The next issue was the days of creation. No issue has been more challenging to fellowship and ministry relationships than this. Being a pastor in conservative evangelicalism in the United States but not a young-earth creationist[7]—how can I describe this? It has felt like attending the University of Tennessee while being a die-hard Georgia fan. It has not been easy. No matter how much you attempt to emphasize the gospel and hold your view graciously, there are some who will always be suspicious

6. Congregationalism is a much smaller part of the church in the United States than it used to be. It did not expand westward as effectively as other denominations, and in later centuries the slide into liberalism was arguably more drastic in Congregationalism than in other segments of the church. For a history of Congregationalism in the United States, and an introduction to the CCCC specifically, see *Modern Day Pilgrims: The First Fifty Years of the Conservative Congregational Christian Conference* (Saint Paul, MN: CCCC, 2000).

7. Young-earth creationism is the view that the days of Genesis 1 are literal, twenty-four-hour solar days, such that the world was created in the relatively recent past.

of you. Unfortunately, the issue of creation days also has led to closed doors of relationship and ministry more than once.

Even in our current church, I received some pointed questions during my candidating weekend about my writings on this topic. Thankfully, we've all managed to get along pretty well together even though a few members hold to a different view of creation than I do. In fact, our church has been wonderfully welcoming and accepting of us, far more than we deserve. But this is another issue that impressed upon me the importance of thinking carefully about theological triage.

Looking Back and Looking Ahead

As I look back on denominational migration, I see God's kindness and provision in the process. But it hasn't been easy. Along the way, I've reflected a lot about when and how doctrine should divide. I don't think I have that all figured out, and I certainly haven't done things perfectly.[8]

But through it all, I have become deeply convinced that in the church we need to do a better job at navigating theological disagreements. Unfortunately, it is common for Christians to divide from one another over relatively insignificant matters. In the worst cases, Christians part ways, often uncharitably, over the most petty and ignorant disagreements. In the other direction, many Christians wink at serious theological error, as if doctrine were unimportant. A balanced attitude about theology is much rarer. We desperately need to cultivate the skills and wisdom to do theological triage so that even when a doctrinal division becomes necessary, it is done with minimal collateral damage to the kingdom of God.

---

8. I may well be wrong about some of these issues I've just recounted. Statistically, it's likely you think so, since the odds are rather slim that you are a fellow nonstrict credobaptist, amillennialist, old-earth creationist, and partial preterist (but if you are, we definitely need to get together and grab whatever beverage your denomination allows).

My great burden in this book is not about baptism, or the days of creation, or the millennium, or any other such issues themselves. If you could get to know me and hear me preach, you would not notice these issues coming up all that frequently. But I am deeply committed to thinking through how these issues and others affect our unity and mission as the church of Jesus Christ. And yes, as I will argue, I do think that some of these issues (especially the days of creation and the millennium) should not be dividing us. I'm also interested in the attitudinal dimension of issues like these. How do we bear our views with winsomeness, humility, and love? Our speech to those outside the church is supposed to be "gracious, seasoned with salt" (Col. 4:6)—surely our speech to those of a different denomination should be too!

Working through doctrinal differences in this way, without compromising either truth or love, will require us to cultivate the skill of ranking the importance of different doctrines. So, in part 2, we consider how we actually *do* theological triage. What are first-rank doctrines? What are second-rank? What are third-rank? And how do we know?

PART 2

THEOLOGICAL TRIAGE AT WORK

4

Why Primary Doctrines Are Worth Fighting For

In theology as well as in battle, some hills are worth dying on. If they are lost, everything is lost. You can get a secondary or tertiary doctrine wrong and still have a fruitful life and ministry—but the denial of a first-rank doctrine is a vital loss.

What makes a first-rank doctrine essential to the gospel? And how do we know what is a first-rank doctrine and what isn't? In this chapter I offer a range of criteria for ranking different doctrines and then articulate two reasons why first-rank doctrines are essential for upholding the gospel, using the virgin birth and justification as examples. These two doctrines provide helpful case studies for why first-rank doctrines are so vital. Here I suggest two overlapping but distinguishable reasons why we should fight for first-rank doctrines:

- Some first-rank doctrines are worth fighting for because they mark a fault line between the gospel and a rival ideology, religion, or worldview (as with the virgin birth).

- Some first-rank doctrines are worth fighting for because they constitute a material point of the gospel (as with justification).

More simply: some first-rank doctrines are needed to *defend* the gospel, and others to *proclaim* the gospel. Without them the gospel is either vulnerable or incomplete.

We could probably articulate more reasons for the importance of first-rank doctrines, and we could certainly list other examples, but hopefully this brief treatment will highlight our need for *courage* and *conviction* in upholding doctrines that are essential to the gospel.

Ranking Different Doctrines

How do we determine how to rank the importance of any particular doctrine? Erik Thoennes offers a helpful list of criteria:

1. Biblical clarity
2. Relevance to the character of God
3. Relevance to the essence of the gospel
4. Biblical frequency and significance (how often in Scripture it is taught, and what weight Scripture places upon it)
5. Effect on other doctrines
6. Consensus among Christians (past and present)
7. Effect on personal and church life
8. Current cultural pressure to deny a teaching of Scripture[1]

A noticeable feature of Thoennes's criteria is the recurring interest in the overall *effect* of a doctrine—on the doctrine of

1. Erik Thoennes, *Life's Biggest Questions: What the Bible Says about the Things That Matter Most* (Wheaton, IL: Crossway, 2011), 35–37.

God (2), on the gospel (3), on other doctrines (5), on the life of the church and individual Christians (7), and so forth. This relates to an important theme of this book: that theological triage is not primarily an intellectual exercise but a practical one. Theological wisdom does not consider doctrines in the abstract, concerned mainly with technical correctness. Instead, it considers doctrines in their "real life" influence on actual people and situations and churches.

For this reason, intelligence and study are not the only or even necessarily the most important factors for doing theological triage well. At least equally important is a desire for godliness and for the flourishing of the church. This practical concern will generate the kinds of instincts that enable godly and wise judgments, and will help us steer away from self-referential considerations, such as our pet peeves, prejudices, and preferences. Even in our theological polemics, we must exhibit a self-restraint that subordinates our personal likes and dislikes to the concerns of the kingdom.

We must also remember that criteria such as those in Thoennes's list function in a cumulative, general way. It is possible for a doctrine to be a first-rank doctrine without necessarily meeting all eight criteria. For instance, the virgin birth is referenced in only a few biblical passages (criterion 4), and yet it qualifies as a first-rank doctrine. Similarly, some doctrines meet several criteria and yet fall short of being first rank. For instance, some doctrines that have been affirmed widely by Christians throughout space and time (criterion 6) do not constitute matters of orthodoxy. Christian views of burial versus cremation might be an example.

Wayne Grudem provides a list of questions that churches and organizations should ask when considering whether to draw a new theological boundary:

1. Certainty: How sure are we that the teaching is wrong?
2. Effect on other doctrines: Will this teaching likely lead to significant erosion in other doctrines?
3. Effect on personal and church life: Will this false teaching bring significant harm to people's Christian lives, or to the work of the church?
4. Historical precedent: Is this teaching contrary to what the vast majority of the Bible-believing church has held throughout history?
5. Perception of importance among God's people: Is there increasing consensus . . . that this matter is important enough that the false teaching should be explicitly denied in a doctrinal statement?
6. Purposes of the organization: Is the teaching a significant threat to the nature and purposes of the organization?
7. Motivations of advocates: Does it seem that the advocates of this teaching hold it because of a fundamental refusal to be subject to the authority of God's Word, rather than because of sincerely held differences of interpretation based on accepted hermeneutical standards?
8. Methods of advocates: Do the advocates of this teaching frequently manifest arrogance, deception, unrighteous anger, slander, and falsehood rather than humility, openness to correction and reason, kindness, and absolute truthfulness?[2]

Grudem's list, like Thoennes's, draws attention to the overall practical effect of a doctrine (especially 2 and 3). We must exhibit caution, of course, with criterion 7, since we cannot ultimately see into the motives of others. Grudem also lists

2. Wayne Grudem, "Why, When, and for What Should We Draw New Boundaries?," in *Beyond the Bounds: Open Theism and the Undermining of Biblical Christianity*, ed. John Piper, Justin Taylor, and Paul Kjoss Helseth (Wheaton, IL: Crossway, 2003), 362–69.

several questions that are wrong to ask and should not be part of the consideration of a particular doctrine:

- Are the advocates my friends?
- Are they nice people?
- Will we lose money or members if we exclude them?
- Will the academic community criticize us as being too narrow-minded?
- Will someone take us to court over this?[3]

These questions draw attention to the danger of losing our objectivity while doing theological triage. An additional question along these lines I would propose is this: "Have I had to fight battles over this doctrine that have affected me personally?" It's easy to exaggerate the importance of a doctrine that has a particular history with you.

The lists given by Grudem and Thoennes are a bit long. For a briefer set of criteria to consider "in a pinch," we might use the following four questions:

1. How clear is *the Bible* on this doctrine?
2. What is this doctrine's importance to *the gospel*?
3. What is the testimony of the *historical church* concerning this doctrine?
4. What is this doctrine's effect upon the *church today*?

These biblical, theological, historical, and practical questions are not all that need be asked, but they are a helpful start for doing theological triage.

Some might wonder how the witness of church history (3) relates to the Reformation principle of *sola Scriptura* (by Scripture alone). The Reformers' appeal to Scripture alone as our only *ultimate* authority was never intended to exclude

3. Grudem, "Why, When, and for What Should We Draw New Boundaries?," 369.

the church's historical testimony from having a lesser, relative authority. It is appropriate and necessary to pursue, for the purposes of doing theological triage, a careful consideration of the wisdom of those who have preceded us in the faith.[4] At the same time, Scripture alone occupies the unique place of final and norming authority. As the Westminster Confession of Faith affirms, "The supreme judge by which all controversies of religion are to be determined, and all decrees of councils, opinions of ancient writers, doctrines of men, and private spirits, are to be examined; and in whose sentence we are to rest; can be no other but the Holy Spirit speaking in the Scripture."[5]

Are First-Rank Doctrines Essential for Salvation?

Sometimes people define essential doctrines as those that must be affirmed in order to experience salvation. In certain circumstances, however, people experience salvation with very limited information. The thief on the cross is a classic example. It is not clear that the thief personally affirmed the Trinity. It seems very likely he did not possess this information in his circumstance. Supposing, for the sake of argument, that this is correct, this would not in itself exclude the Trinity from being a first-rank doctrine.

Several distinctions can help us in this regard. First, we should distinguish between what must *be affirmed* and what must *not be denied*.[6] Some Christians will lack the mental capacity, theological awareness, or communicative ability to

4. I develop this claim more fully in Gavin Ortlund, "*Sola Scriptura* Then and Now: Biblical Authority in Late Medieval and Reformation Context," *Credo* 6, no. 4 (December 2016); available online January 31, 2017, https://credomag.com/2017/01/sola-scriptura-then-and-now-biblical-authority-in-late-medieval-and-reformation-context/.

5. The Westminster Confession of Faith, 1.10.

6. On this point, see Michael E. Wittmer, *Don't Stop Believing: Why Living Like Jesus Is Not Enough* (Grand Rapids, MI: Zondervan, 2008), 43.

express various first-rank doctrines. For instance, would you require an eight-year-old to positively articulate the relation of the divine and human natures of Christ before you accepted his faith as sincere? Of course not. But these are still first-rank doctrines; they are implicit in any confession of the gospel, and they must not be denied.

Related to this, we must distinguish between what must be affirmed *when someone becomes a Christian* and what must be affirmed *as characteristic of growth in Christ over time*. It would be unhelpful to require that every Christian affirm every first-rank doctrine at the moment of his or her conversion. In real life, people often come to Christ without hearing about every first-rank doctrine, and they grow in their understanding of these doctrines over time (hopefully more quickly than slowly).

In addition, when a first-rank doctrine is denied, we must distinguish between a denial based upon ignorance or confusion and a knowing, willful denial. Sincere Christians can have partial or muddled understandings of various first-rank doctrines, and therefore imperfect statements, prayers, and affirmations related to them. Most of us have heard a prayer thanking God the Father for dying on the cross. This is technically the ancient heresy called patripassianism, rejected by the early church; but it would be a massive pastoral blunder to declare someone a heretic for making this mistake. We must distinguish between confused sheep and active wolves.

Is there ever a time when a true Christian denies a first-rank doctrine? How much error may we tolerate before losing confidence in someone's salvation? It is difficult to say. The heart often has better theology than the brain. In this chapter I will identify the virgin birth as essential; but I make no judgment that Emil Brunner (who denied it) was unregenerate. Judgments about the personal salvation of others are precarious. We do not see into the heart. We do not know a person's final thoughts and ultimate decisions. Judgment is ultimately God's to exercise, and it is wise for us to be cautious.

Rather than insisting on a positive articulation of every first-rank doctrine for salvation, a more careful statement would be that if someone knowingly and persistently denies a first-rank tenet, we can have no confidence of that person's salvation. But it would probably be better to restrict our focus to whether we would allow such a person into the membership of our church than to speculate about the state of his or her soul. It is God's business to regulate entry to heaven, and ours to regulate entry to the church. As Herman Witsius put it long ago: "It may not be safe and expedient for us to receive into church-fellowship, a person chargeable with some error or sin; whom, however, we should not dare, on account of that error or sin, to exclude from heaven."[7]

The Virgin Birth

The virgin birth is not the doctrinal flashpoint today that it was during the fundamentalist-modernist controversy, when it came under fire along with other "fundamentals" of the Christian faith, following the rise of higher-critical biblical scholarship and theological liberalism. Nonetheless, it can serve as an example of a first-rank doctrine that is essential to the defense of the gospel against rival ideologies or worldviews. In 1930, J. Gresham Machen offered a substantive defense of the virgin birth based on a variety of historical, textual, and theological considerations.[8] The historical argument that N. T. Wright has

7. Herman Witsius, *Sacred Dissertations on the Apostles' Creed*, trans. Donald Fraser, vol. 1 (Grand Rapids, MI: Reformation Heritage Books, 2010), 28–29.

8. J. Gresham Machen, *The Virgin Birth of Christ* (1930; repr., Grand Rapids, MI: Baker, 1965).

made more recently about the resurrection (namely, that its sudden emergence in history commends its plausibility) Machen was making almost a century ago with respect to the virgin birth.

After his four-hundred-page defense of the virgin birth, Machen came to "the last question with which it is necessary for us to deal—the question, namely, as to the importance of the virgin birth to the Christian man."[9] Machen's answer provides us with a helpful model for how to do theological triage on first-rank doctrines. Though we are in a different context, the principles involved in Machen's defense remain highly relevant and useful.

In the first place, Machen distinguished between affirming the virgin birth and affirming it *as a first-rank doctrine*. He recognized that in his day "there are many who tell us that, though they believe in the virgin birth themselves, they do not think that that belief is important for all men or essential even to the corporate witness of the Church."[10] In contrast to this approach, Machen argued that the virgin birth is not a matter of private judgment but is essential to the church's worship, witness, and vitality. To support this claim, he developed three considerations.

First, Machen claimed that the virgin birth is "obviously important for the general question of the authority of the Bible."[11] After all, even among those who deny the virgin birth, it is generally admitted that the Bible affirms this doctrine. Thus, the differences result not from different interpretations of the relevant passages but from a different construal of the nature of biblical authority. Machen therefore argued that a denial of the virgin birth compromises an adequate doctrine of Scripture.[12]

9. Machen, *Virgin Birth of Christ*, 382.
10. Machen, *Virgin Birth of Christ*, 382.
11. Machen, *Virgin Birth of Christ*, 382.
12. Machen, *Virgin Birth of Christ*, 382–87.

Second, Machen argued that the virgin birth is important "as a test for a man to apply to himself or to others to determine whether one holds a naturalistic or a supernaturalistic view regarding Jesus Christ."[13] Machen recognized that to deny the virgin birth is not necessarily to deny the supernatural; nor does affirming the virgin birth necessarily imply affirming all of Christianity. Nonetheless, he saw the virgin birth as a particularly helpful litmus test to distinguish orthodox Christology from revisionist views of modernists who affirm Christ's "deity" and "resurrection" while meaning something altogether different by these terms.[14]

Finally, Machen insisted that the virgin birth has an intrinsic importance, such that "without the story of the virgin birth there would be something seriously lacking in the Christian view of Christ."[15] The virgin birth is an organic part of the whole Christian message of Jesus, and it signals and protects its supernatural character. Specifically, Machen suggested that the virgin birth protects us against various Christological heresies, enables us to uphold a full doctrine of the incarnation, and guards and illumines the nature of Jesus's sinlessness.[16]

Machen did not go so far as to insist that an affirmation of the virgin birth is essential for personal salvation. "Who can tell exactly how much knowledge of the facts about Christ is necessary if a man is to have saving faith? None but God can tell."[17] Nonetheless, Machen distinguished between what we must affirm for individual salvation and what we must affirm for the health of the church in our generation: "Even if the virgin birth is not necessary to every Christian, it is certainly necessary to Christianity."[18]

13. Machen, *Virgin Birth of Christ*, 387.
14. Machen, *Virgin Birth of Christ*, 387–91.
15. Machen, *Virgin Birth of Christ*, 392.
16. Machen, *Virgin Birth of Christ*, 394–95.
17. Machen, *Virgin Birth of Christ*, 395.
18. Machen, *Virgin Birth of Christ*, 396.

Machen's carefulness on this point encourages us to consider some fine distinctions in the consideration of first-rank doctrines. It may be possible, strictly speaking, to affirm the incarnation without affirming the virgin birth—and yet the denial of the virgin birth does vital damage to our view of the incarnation. As F. F. Bruce wrote:

> There are those, indeed, who acknowledge our Lord's incarnation without believing in His virgin birth, just as others, Muslims for example, believe in His virgin birth but not in His incarnation. But it is undeniable that His incarnation and virgin birth are intimately bound together in the historic faith of the church.[19]

Bruce drew attention to how the uniqueness of the incarnation itself signals the fittingness and even inevitability that the *means* of Christ's incarnation should be unique among human births.[20] Accordingly, Bruce quoted with approval the conclusion of W. R. Matthews: "Though we may still believe in the Incarnation without the Virgin Birth, it will not be precisely the same kind of Incarnation, and the conception of God's act of redemption in Christ will be subtly but definitely changed."[21]

Machen's treatment of the virgin birth can help us reflect upon the importance of first-rank doctrines today. In the first place, he drew attention to the way first-rank doctrines often relate to the role of biblical authority in our theology. Although many differences in the realm of secondary and tertiary doctrines boil down to differing interpretations among those who uphold the authority of Scripture, the acceptance or rejection of a first-rank doctrine is often part and parcel of

19. F. F. Bruce, "The Person of Christ: Incarnation and Virgin Birth," in *Basic Christian Doctrines*, ed. Carl F. H. Henry (New York: Holt, Rinehart, and Winston, 1962), 128.
20. Bruce, "Person of Christ," 128.
21. Bruce, "Person of Christ," 129–30.

the acceptance or rejection of Scripture itself (whether this is admitted or not).

Biblical authority is one of the most pressing issues for the life and health of the church: it ensures that we remain the judged, not the judges, in our relation to God and truth. It is easy, even while having a notionally high view of the Bible, to let some other ideology or value filter which parts of the Bible *function* authoritatively over us. A healthy Christian will be continually corrected and repaired by God's word, and will submit to—even delight in—this correcting process. One reason first-rank doctrines are worth fighting for is that their denial weakens the authoritative, corrective role that God's word is supposed to have over us.

As an extension of Machen's second point, we may observe that a frequent characteristic of first-rank doctrines is that they are bound up with larger worldview conflicts between historic Christianity and current heresies or fads. The gospel is always in conflict with "spirits of the age." In Machen's day, for instance, the virgin birth was one of the points at which historic Christianity, as taught in Scripture and understood by the consensus of Christians throughout church history, was under attack by a rival religious view (namely, modernism with its antisupernatural presuppositions).

There will be comparable situations in every generation. The truth is unchanging, but culture is constantly changing; so there will always be points of friction between truth and culture. One reason first-rank doctrines are worth fighting for is that their defense is often bound up with the defense of the gospel, as understood through the ages, at its point of current attack. Hence, first-rank doctrines are often those which have been affirmed by Christians of various denominations and traditions throughout history; they are often either explicit or at least implicit in ecumenical creeds and councils; they often fit within the parameters of what C. S. Lewis called "mere Christianity."

Finally, in line with how Machen (and Bruce) explained the relation of the virgin birth and the gospel, we may say that first-rank doctrines often have such a close and intimate relationship to the gospel that if they are denied, the gospel itself is ruptured. This relationship can be complicated—not every first-rank doctrine is equally important to the gospel, or important to the gospel in the same way. For instance, my defense of justification below will press this point more than I have here with the virgin birth. But the denial of a first-rank doctrine is *never* a matter of neutrality to the gospel. In some way or another, first-rank doctrines are always important to a robust and healthy witness to the gospel.

Justification by Faith Alone

The Protestant Reformers held justification by faith alone to be essential to the gospel. In fact, it is difficult to exaggerate how much they emphasized this point. As Philip Ryken summarizes:

> John Calvin called [justification] "the main hinge on which salvation turns." The English Reformer Thomas Cranmer described it as "the strong rock and foundation of Christian religion." Perhaps most famously of all, Martin Luther called justification "the chief article of Christian doctrine," so that "when justification has fallen, everything has fallen."[22]

All this would seem to signal justification as a quintessential first-rank issue. But at the outset we are confronted with the difficulty that godly Christians have disagreed about justification. A clear distinction between what Protestants typically call

22. Philip Graham Ryken, "Justification," in *The Gospel as Center: Renewing Our Faith and Reforming Our Ministry Practices*, ed. D. A. Carson and Timothy Keller (Wheaton, IL: Crossway, 2012), 153–54.

justification (the initial declaration of our righteous status) and sanctification (our continual growth in righteousness throughout the Christian life) was absent for much of the early and medieval church. Saint Augustine, for example, thought of justification as involving both of these realities and would not have separated our being *declared* righteous from our being *made* righteous in the way the Reformers did.[23] Or, even in the Protestant tradition, one can find Christians, like Richard Baxter, who deny the concept of double imputation (affirming, instead, that the forgiveness of sins is imputed to believers but not the righteousness of Christ) and conceive of justification as a process.[24] It is easy to exaggerate differences among Christians on the topic of justification, but it is indisputable that they exist.

Thus, in dealing with the doctrine of justification as a first-rank doctrine, we must remember that this doctrine has various components, and each component is not necessarily as important as the whole. When I affirm justification by faith alone as a first-rank doctrine, I am dealing with a kind of "mere" justification by faith alone, not with this doctrine in all its nuances. In other words, I am dealing with the basic fact that our right standing before God is on terms of grace and is received not by any merit. Such an affirmation can be made by those who parse differently the exact nature of imputation of Christ's active and passive righteousness, or take different views on the New Perspective on Paul, or feel differently about Protestant-Catholic differences after, say, the 1999 Joint Declaration or the second Evangelicals and Catholics Together publication.[25] These are all

23. Alister E. McGrath, Iustitia Dei*: A History of the Christian Doctrine of Justification*, 3rd ed. (Cambridge: Cambridge University Press, 2005), 31.

24. Thomas Schreiner, *Faith Alone: The Doctrine of Justification*, The 5 Solas (Grand Rapids, MI: Zondervan, 2015), 76–77, draws attention to some of the nuances in Baxter's view.

25. These documents indicate that the Catholic doctrine of justification has moved closer toward a Protestant one—though while *sola fide* is affirmed in principle, impu-

important issues, but for our purposes here, I am focusing on the more basic claim that our rightness before God is by grace apart from merit.

In this discussion we must also keep in mind, in line with our previous discussion, that the affirmation of a doctrine is not necessarily the same as the studied, self-aware articulation of that doctrine. Therefore, the fact that someone does not verbally affirm justification by faith alone does not necessarily mean that in that person's heart and conscience he or she is not trusting in Christ for justification. As John Owen observed, "Men may be really saved by that grace which doctrinally they do deny; and they may be justified by the imputation of that righteousness which in opinion they deny to be imputed."[26]

Tom Schreiner provides a model of someone who defends a traditionally Reformed account of justification and yet is irenic and generous in his consideration of points of dispute. He cautions us against too rashly categorizing someone on the basis of the affirmation or rejection of one particular word or slogan; we must listen carefully so that we understand what an opposing view really entails. As he warns, "Those who reject the motto [*sola fide*] aren't necessarily proclaiming a different gospel."[27]

But where does justification stand in the overall scheme of Christian theology? On the one hand, it is possible to overcentralize justification. Some Lutheran theologians, for example, have conceived of justification as the complete subject matter of theology, or the criterion for every theological

tation remains a point of dispute, as well as the general soteriological context of the Catholic doctrine of justification, with its view of purgatory, penance, etc.

26. John Owen, "The Doctrine of Justification by Faith through the Imputation of the Righteousness of Christ; Explained, Confirmed, and Vindicated," in *The Works of John Owen*, ed. William H. Goold, vol. 5 (Carlisle, PA: Banner of Truth, 1965), 164.

27. Schreiner, *Faith Alone*, 18.

statement.[28] It's difficult to know how to reconcile such views with the biblical presentation of justification, which situates justification in the context of other doctrines without which justification loses its meaning.[29] In the opposite direction, however, it would be a mistake to think of justification as simply one more blessing of the gospel, on equal footing with all the others. Michael Allen displays a healthy balance in assigning justification a privileged place among aspects of the gospel without thereby making it the center of all Christian theology. As he has put it, "Justification is not merely a discrete component of the whole, but . . . is a constituent aspect of the whole."[30] We might say that justification is not, in itself, the whole gospel; but it nonetheless *touches* the whole gospel.

Why should justification hold such a special place within Christian theology? We could answer this question many ways, but here I'll consider how often in the New Testament the apostles are willing to fight over justification by faith alone. There are many topics the apostles *don't* fight over but on which they instead call for our forbearance and moderation (see, e.g., Rom. 14; 1 Cor. 8). The topics that generate polemics, by contrast, are relatively rare. Craig Blomberg lists four kinds of errors that the New Testament most strongly opposes: (1) any denial of the full humanity and deity of Christ; (2) any denial of salvation by grace through faith (either through some form of legalism, nomism, or ethnocentrism or through antinomianism); (3) the denial of the future bodily return of Christ; and (4) various distortions of the doctrine of sanctification, such as

28. Michael Allen, *Justification and the Gospel: Understanding the Contexts and Controversies* (Grand Rapids, MI: Baker Academic, 2013), 8–9, summarizes and analyzes several claims made to this effect by Oswald Bayer and Mark Mattes, as well as Webster's response.

29. Richard B. Gaffin Jr., *Resurrection and Redemption: A Study in Paul's Soteriology* (Phillipsburg, NJ: Presbyterian and Reformed, 1987), provides a powerful argument that union with Christ is the organizing linchpin of Paul's conception of salvation.

30. Allen, *Justification and the Gospel*, 12.

defeatism or triumphalism.[31] It is striking how much energy is generated in the New Testament over the second of these four issues: theological errors that amount to a denial of grace.

For instance, there is no more polemical book in the New Testament than Galatians. In every other letter, Paul opens by thanking God for the faith of those he is addressing—even when there are gross errors in the church, such as the Corinthian believers' getting drunk at the Lord's Supper (1 Cor. 11:21). But to the Galatian Christians, Paul opens with rebuke: "I am astonished that you are so quickly deserting him who called you in the grace of Christ and are turning to a different gospel" (Gal. 1:6). Paul then offers an anathema on all, including angels, who preach a different gospel than the one they have received:

> Even if we or an angel from heaven should preach to you a gospel contrary to the one we preached to you, let him be accursed. As we have said before, so now I say again: If anyone is preaching to you a gospel contrary to the one you received, let him be accursed. (Gal. 1:8–9)

Why is Paul's tone to the Galatians so strident? What is this "different gospel" being presented to them? After recounting his apostolic calling to the gospel, Paul identifies the root issue, drawing from his confrontation with Peter: "A person is not justified by works of the law but through faith in Jesus Christ, so we also have believed in Christ Jesus, in order to be justified by faith in Christ and not by works of the law, because by works of the law no one will be justified" (Gal. 2:16). Here Paul stipulates, strikingly, that the acceptance of justification by works entails a rejection of the gospel. Thus, for Paul, maintaining justification by faith alone is necessary in order to be

31. Craig Blomberg, "The New Testament Definition of Heresy (or When Do Jesus and the Apostles Really Get Mad?)," *Journal of the Evangelical Theological Society* 45, no. 1 (March 2002): 71.

faithful to Christ and uphold his gospel. To waver on this point is to fall away from Christ himself. Paul, in fact, warns the Galatians that they have been "severed from Christ" (Gal. 5:4).

The book of Galatians reminds us that there are hills to die on and that justification by faith alone is one of those hills. Again, there are nuances involved in the doctrine of justification that genuine Christians can disagree on. But the fundamental claim that we are right with God by faith in Christ alone, apart from our good works—this is integral to the gospel and to every practical aspect of the Christian life. For instance, it bears directly upon how we relate to God on a daily basis, how we worship him, how we fight sin in our lives, and how we function as the church. John Berridge linked justification with the doctrine of regeneration as vital to the church's health:

> When the doctrines of regeneration and justification by faith become despised or deserted doctrines, the labors of the clergy will prove useless, their persons will grow cheap, their office will seem contemptible, and they at length may be ashamed of their *function* and their *livery*.[32]

J. I. Packer made a similar observation with respect to church history:

> When this doctrine [justification by faith] is understood, believed, and preached, as it was in New Testament times, the church stands in the grace of God and is alive; but where it is neglected, overlaid, or denied, as it was in medieval Catholicism, the church falls from grace and its life drains away, leaving it in a state of darkness and death.[33]

---

32. John Berridge, *The Christian World Unmasked* (Boston: Gould and Lincoln, 1854), 180.

33. J. I. Packer, introduction to James Buchanan, *The Doctrine of Justification: An Outline of Its History in the Church and of Its Exposition from Scripture* (1867; repr., London: Banner of Truth, 1961), 1.

Packer's comment, however, raises a question. Is justification by faith alone really a catholic doctrine if it was lost to the church for so many generations prior to the Reformation? This is a valid concern insofar as the witness of church history is an important, though not final, consideration in theological triage (recall Thoennes's criterion 6 and Grudem's 4).

However, the different understandings of justification through church history are easy to exaggerate. To be sure, gross abuses of the doctrine have occurred, such as in the late medieval church when the sale of indulgences and other abuses pertaining to justification became rampant. Thomas Oden, however, has marshaled evidence of a wide consensus throughout classical Christianity that salvation comes by grace through faith.[34] Well before Oden, others made a similar claim, including some of the firmest advocates for a Reformed doctrine of justification. James Buchanan, for example, although acknowledging corruptions and imperfections in the church's understanding of justification, insisted that true believers were "nourished and refreshed by [this doctrine], even in the darkest and most degenerate times."[35] Concluding his historical survey, he claimed that "the Protestant doctrine of Justification by grace through faith was not a novelty introduced into the Church by Luther and Calvin. . . . There is no truth in the allegation that it had been unknown for fourteen hundred years before the Reformation."[36] While we should be careful not to downplay differences on justification throughout church history, the core meaning of this doctrine has been surprisingly resilient.

---

34. Thomas C. Oden, *The Justification Reader* (Grand Rapids, MI: Eerdmans, 2002); Oden, *Classic Christianity: A Systematic Theology* (New York: HarperOne, 1992), 583–622.
35. Buchanan, *Doctrine of Justification*, 93.
36. Buchanan, *Doctrine of Justification*, 111.

Hills Worth Fighting For

Our theology must have a category for the censorious tone of Paul's letter to the Galatians and the grit and resolve of Machen's polemics. We must not reduce gospel witness to a generic niceness that is accommodating in every circumstance. There is a time to fight. There are certain hills that must not be surrendered, even if the cost is losing our lives.

Many of us do not prefer, as a matter of temperament, theological polemics. We would rather preach the gospel than refute error. That is commendable as a matter of preference. Consider the way Jude expresses it: "Although I was very *eager* to write to you about our common salvation, I found it *necessary* to write appealing to you to contend for the faith that was once for all delivered to the saints" (Jude 3). Celebrating the gospel should be a matter of *eagerness*; contending for it, a matter of *necessity*. Regrettably, for some Christians it is the reverse.

But celebrating the faith will also require, eventually, contending for it. No one can avoid confronting error forever. For Paul, it was the first-century Judaizers; for Machen, the twentieth-century modernists; there will be something for us. The gospel is simply too controversial, too disruptive, *not* to be attacked. As Machen noted, "In the sphere of religion, as in other spheres, the things about which men are agreed are apt to be the things that are least worth holding; the really important things are the things about which men will fight."[37] Therefore, there can be no effective, long-term ministry of the gospel without a corresponding willingness to engage in its defense.

Are there hills we are willing to die on? Are we willing to take a stand, come what may, on those doctrines that separate the gospel from the spirit of the age? If not, we are not faithful servants of Christ, and will not be effective in advancing his kingdom.

37. J. Gresham Machen, *Christianity and Liberalism* (New York: Macmillan, 1923), 1–2.

5

Navigating the Complexity of Secondary Doctrines

In chapter 4, I argued that the appropriate mentality corresponding to first-rank doctrines is *courage and conviction*. In chapter 6, I will argue that the appropriate mentality regarding third-rank doctrines is *circumspection and restraint*. Here I propose that our mentality concerning second-rank doctrines should be *wisdom and balance*.

By "second-rank doctrines" I mean that middle body of Christian doctrines that make a noticeable difference in how we understand and articulate the gospel, though their denial does not generally constitute a denial of the gospel. Second-rank doctrines are not essential to the gospel, but they are often important enough to justify divisions at the level of denomination, church, or ministry. These are issues outside the Apostles' Creed but more important than, say, your interpretation of an obscure passage in Daniel.

In this chapter I want to draw attention to two broad and somewhat overlapping reasons for the importance of secondary doctrines. First, although second-rank doctrines are not essential to the gospel, they exert a significant influence over our witness to and/or our understanding of the gospel. Second, second-rank doctrines lead to practical differences in how we do church and/or ministry, such that attempting formal unity amid our different convictions will often lead to divisiveness, confusion, and violations of conscience. For these reasons, it is understandable and appropriate—though ultimately regrettable—that Christians divide over these issues in certain contexts.

I will touch upon three second-rank doctrines that tend to be controversial among evangelicals: (1) baptism (particularly credobaptism versus paedobaptism), (2) spiritual gifts (particularly cessationism versus continuationism), and (3) women in ministry (particularly complementarianism versus egalitarianism). My treatment of these issues will be all too brief, and I make no effort to resolve them. Rather, my goal is to show why these doctrinal disputes are broadly in the second-rank doctrinal range, and to encourage learning, cooperation, clarity, and awareness in how we engage doctrines like these.

This chapter is the most difficult and complicated of the whole book. I am acutely aware that I am making fallible judgment calls in what follows. I am also aware that I am to some extent limiting my comments to contexts I am familiar with. But I offer these evaluations in the hope that they will serve others who are finding their way through secondary doctrines, even if their circumstances or convictions differ from what I outline here. If this chapter does nothing more than to prompt reflection on the complexity of doing theological triage on second-rank doctrines and encourage us toward prayer, humility, and study, it will have served a purpose.

Why Secondary Doctrines Can Be Hard to Rank

Some doctrines are easy to rank—I have no hesitation in labeling the doctrine of the Trinity, for instance, a first-rank doctrine. It is foundational to the gospel; its essential content is clearly and abundantly set forth in the Bible; it was systematically defined by the early ecumenical creeds and councils; and it is practically relevant throughout every aspect of the Christian life.

But, of course, not every doctrine fits neatly into one of three or four categories. There is a *spectrum* of doctrinal importance. Some doctrines, we might conclude, are on the border between one category and another. For instance, some secondary doctrines might be *almost* essential; others might be *almost* tertiary. Thus, if we assume that all secondary doctrines are *equally* secondary, we may be in danger of glossing over important differences.

This is a danger inherent in any system of categorization. It is not a reason to avoid the use of categories; it just means we must recognize that they are somewhat clunky and inexact and therefore do not convey all that must be said about a doctrine. Oversimplification is a particular risk with second-rank doctrines. They are distinctive in that they fall short of being essential to the gospel, but they are important enough to separate Christians from one another. By definition, therefore, this category spans a wide breadth of issues, whereas first-rank and third-rank doctrines are arguably more focused categories.

I am especially eager to help people avoid thinking like this: "X is a second-rank issue; y is a second-rank issue; therefore, x and y are equally important." If you tell me a doctrine is secondary, you have told me something about its importance but not everything. Generally speaking, you have told me relatively little.

There are several other reasons why second-rank doctrines are difficult to categorize, and why we must therefore examine each of them with sensitivity to its context and its relation to the whole gospel. First, doctrines do not exist in a theological vacuum. Each doctrine finds its ultimate meaning in relation to the entire gospel. Thus, some doctrines may appear to be relatively minor in themselves but utterly essential in the way they function toward other doctrines—like a plank in a bridge that looks relatively unimportant but in fact keeps it from collapsing. As an example, many modern Christians reject the idea that God is simple because they find it bizarre, without consideration of how foundational this doctrine has been throughout church history for grounding a proper conception of God's transcendence over the world.

Second, the importance of any particular doctrine sometimes turns out to depend, to some extent, on context and usage. As I have indicated, being a member in a church and being an elder in a church should have different doctrinal criteria. Or a particular doctrine may be especially urgent for the church's public witness at one time and place, and less so at another. That doesn't mean that the truth of the doctrine itself ever changes; but if you are doing triage, you might look at these issues differently, depending on the level of practical urgency at play.

Finally, when we engage in theological triage, we are dealing not just with doctrines but also with doctrinal attitudes. Every Christian, church, ministry, and theological institution has not only theological positions but also a theological culture or ethos—a set of unspoken tendencies and unofficial policies. Often what causes division is not a breach of any official statement of faith but a conflict at the level of ethos and culture.

Theological triage is, therefore, about far more than technical correctness in adjudicating this or that doctrine. It involves our whole posture toward theology. As one of the pastors I interviewed put it to me, having observed the lack of love Christians often exhibit amid doctrinal differences, "It's not just about what you fight over but about how you fight."[1] We must especially bear this point in mind when dealing with secondary doctrines.

Baptism

One of the most divisive areas of theology throughout church history has been the sacraments. How many are there: two? seven? What should we call them ("ordinances" or "sacraments")? How, if at all, do they convey the grace of God to us; are they effectual apart from faith? To whom should they be administered, and by whom, and how frequently?

Disagreements about such questions have been going on throughout church history. For instance, the question of the manner of Christ's presence in the Lord's Supper, which prevented the union of the Lutheran and Reformed branches of the Reformation at Marburg in 1529, was in its broad form a leading debate in the ninth-century church between Radbertus and Ratramnus, and continued to create controversy through the medieval period (e.g., in the eleventh century, Berengar of Tours was disciplined for questioning the official doctrine on this same point). Since Luther and Zwingli's famous disagreement, this question has continued to divide Protestants, as have related questions about the Lord's Supper (e.g., the question of who should be admitted to the Lord's Supper was the presenting issue in Jonathan Edwards's dismissal from his church).

One of the most painful sources of division in the body of Christ, from the Protestant Reformation to the present day, has

1. Hans Kristensen, who ministers in Sydney, Australia, put this helpful observation to me during a March 2019 Skype conversation.

concerned the proper subjects of the sacrament (or ordinance) of baptism. Should only those who make a credible profession of faith be baptized, or are the children of one or more believing parents also proper subjects of Christian baptism?

Historically, Christians have not only divided from one another over this issue—they have killed one another. The Diet of Speyer in 1529—where the word "Protestant" was first used—decreed that "every Anabaptist or rebaptized person, of either sex, is to be put to death, by fire or by sword, or by some other means."[2] Many Anabaptists were also, in a bitter twist of irony, drowned. The perpetrators were not just Roman Catholic authorities but also Reformation voices like Ulrich Zwingli. The first Anabaptist martyr had been Felix Manz, who in 1526 had been bound and submerged in the icy waters of the river Limmat in Zurich, just a few hundred yards from Zwingli's church. Zwingli had reportedly said, "Let him who talks about going under [the water] go under."[3]

All told, there were probably more Anabaptist martyrs in the sixteenth century than Christian martyrs in the first three centuries of the church, prior to the conversion of Constantine.[4] Let that sink in: more Christians were killed *by each other over baptism* during the Reformation than were killed by the Roman Empire over their faith in Christ.

Part of the reason baptism has generated such virulent fighting is that it is tied to larger questions concerning the nature of the church and—after Constantine's conversion and prior to the rise of modernity—the nature and structure of society itself.

2. Quoted in Erwin Lutzer, *The Doctrines That Divide: A Fresh Look at the Historical Doctrines That Separate Christians* (Grand Rapids, MI: Kregel, 1989), 125.

3. Quoted in John H. Armstrong, "Introduction: Division, Differences, and a Dream," in *Understanding Four Views on Baptism*, ed. John H. Armstrong, Counterpoints (Grand Rapids, MI: Zondervan, 2007), 19.

4. Justo L. González, *The Story of Christianity*, vol. 2, *The Reformation to the Present Day* (New York: HarperCollins, 1985), 56.

The Anabaptists were seen as a threat to the social fabric that held Christendom together.

We approach the topic of baptism differently today, living in a late-modern context in which (for most of us) church and state are separated. This is especially the case when we are dealing with covenantal paedobaptism, the species of paedobaptism among Reformed and Presbyterian Christians, rather than varieties of paedobaptism that include a notion of baptismal regeneration. Baptismal regeneration assigns saving efficacy to the administration of baptism, typically seeing it as an instrumental means of regeneration. This has been the dominant form of paedobaptism throughout church history, and it is espoused today by Catholicism, Orthodoxy, and (in one variety or another) by many of the major Protestant denominations, such as Anglicanism and Lutheranism.

Those who reject the notion of baptismal regeneration protest that the whole point of baptism is to point us *toward* Jesus Christ in his saving benefits in the gospel, accessed by faith and repentance. In contexts where baptism is understood as entrance to both the society and the church all at once, and in which baptism is assigned some kind of saving efficacy, baptism can often have the opposite effect, pointing us away from the need for personal faith and putting our confidence in the power of the ritual itself. This is a constant danger with the sacraments—that the outer rite replaces, rather than spotlights, the inner reality of which it is a symbol.

This concern, of course, can be equally held by credobaptists and paedobaptists alike. In fact, among the fiercest critics of indiscriminate baptism and sacramentalist[5] abuse are

5. Sacramentalism is the belief in the necessity and efficacy of the sacraments for salvation.

paedobaptists. Søren Kierkegaard, who himself affirmed infant baptism as "the anticipation of a possibility," nonetheless railed against its abuse in the Danish Lutheran state church for giving the impression that everyone in the society was a Christian simply by being baptized. He remarked:

> The Christianity of "Christendom" sees that everything depends upon establishing the maxim that one becomes a Christian as a child, that if one is rightly to become a Christian, one must be such from *infancy. This is the basic falsehood. If this is put through, then good night to the Christianity of the New Testament.*[6]

Moreover, some credobaptist groups embrace various forms of sacramentalism.[7] Thus, questions concerning the proper *subjects* of baptism are complicated by larger questions concerning the meaning and usage of baptism. In light of this, a one-size-fits-all evaluation of theological triage cannot be made about credobaptism or paedobaptism. We need wisdom to evaluate the practice of baptism in any particular group or denomination, taking into account the overall effect of the practice on the church and the gospel.

How shall we think about baptism in theological triage? In the first place, we must be careful not to react against the ugliness that is a tragic part of our history by swinging in the opposite direction and declaring baptism of no importance at all. There are several reasons why we must earnestly uphold the importance of baptism.

---

6. *The Instant*, no. 7, "The Formula of 'Christendom,'" *Attack upon Christendom*, 212, as cited in Paul K. Jewett, *Infant Baptism and the Covenant of Grace: An Appraisal of the Argument That as Infants Were Once Circumcised So They Should Now Be Baptized* (Grand Rapids, MI: Eerdmans, 1978), 243, Jewett's emphasis.

7. For example, the Churches of Christ, which practice credobaptism, understand baptism to mark an integral and necessary part of the conversion process. For a fuller explanation, see John D. Castelein, "Christian Churches/Churches of Christ View," in Armstrong, *Understanding Four Views on Baptism*, 129–44.

First, baptism is a matter of obedience to Christ. It was instituted by Jesus (Matt. 28:19–20), and Jesus himself was baptized, stipulating its necessity to "fulfill all righteousness" (Matt. 3:15). People today often think of baptism as fundamentally a matter of "expressing my faith," and elevate the experiential aspect of being baptized.[8] While baptism is certainly an expression of faith, and the experience of being baptized is a profound blessing, it is also more. Ultimately, baptism is a matter of discipleship, a sort of "crossing of the Rubicon" moment when a person becomes publicly identified as a follower of Christ. For example, in many parts of the world, baptism marks the point at which Christians become targets for persecution. A pastor in Singapore whom I interviewed as part of my research for this book shared with me that in his context, parents often allow their children to go to his church without much concern, but when the children want to be baptized, there is a much stronger backlash.[9] Similarly, Christians in China will often be allowed to read their Bibles and even worship Jesus, but pursuing baptism will result in persecution.[10]

Second, baptism plays an important role in our corporate life together as the people of God. Baptism is the official visible marker of entry into the church and therefore ultimately corresponds to the boundaries of church membership. Therefore, our doctrine of baptism is profoundly related to our doctrine of the church. Too often in our individualistic society we think

8. On this point, paedobaptists often do better than credobaptists. Credobaptists often make baptism a sign of faith, rather than a sign of Christ. Sinclair Ferguson, "Infant Baptist View," in *Baptism: Three Views*, ed. David F. Wright (Downers Grove, IL: IVP Academic, 2009), 96, puts it well: "Baptism is first and foremost a Christocentric emblem, not a fidecentric one."

9. Simon Murphy, lead pastor of Redemption Hill Church in Singapore, shared this observation with me on March 31, 2019.

10. Daniel G. Reid, introduction to Wright, *Baptism: Three Views*, 13, relates this observation, put to him by an Asian theologian.

of baptism as a private experience and overlook the corporate function it is designed to play among the people of God.

Third, baptism is given to the church not merely as a boundary marker but also as a sign and seal of the gospel itself. The water portrays the washing away of sins (Acts 22:16), and the immersion into water symbolizes union with Christ in his death, burial, and resurrection (Rom. 6:3–4). Therefore, rather than seeing baptism simply as an individual's public statement of faith (which it surely is), baptism should also be seen as one way the church bears witness to the gospel. This means that baptism is intended as a blessing not just to the person being baptized but also to the entire church family that observes the baptism. When we witness a baptism, we receive a visible portrait of what Christ has accomplished for us in his life, death, and resurrection on our behalf. Baptism is, in the words of Timothy George, "a central liturgical act of Christian worship."[11]

While we should not downplay baptism, it would also be a mistake to elevate it to a first-rank issue alongside the gospel. Baptism does not set the boundaries of orthodoxy, such that those who get it right are orthodox and those who get it wrong are heretics. The difference between a Baptist and a Presbyterian is not the same as the difference between a Christian and a heretic. Baptism does not wield that level of importance because it is not a doctrine on which the gospel is won or lost. Christians on both sides of the baptism debate can have lives and ministry that are fruitful for the gospel. Strikingly, the apostle Paul even subordinated his calling to baptize under his calling to preach the gospel: "Christ did not send me to baptize but to preach the gospel" (1 Cor. 1:17). Thus, we should avoid making baptism

11. Timothy George, foreword to *Believer's Baptism: Sign of the New Covenant in Christ*, ed. Thomas R. Schreiner and Shawn D. Wright, NAC Studies in Bible and Theology (Nashville: B&H, 2006), xvii.

an identity issue for who is "safe," or regard those with whom we disagree as ignorant or rebellious, or restrict our Christian fellowship and partnership in the gospel to those who share our view.

We need wisdom today to hold our convictions about baptism without compromise and yet to maintain unity and fellowship, as much as we can, with Christians who hold different convictions than we do. How do we balance these two concerns? This is no easy question, and I cannot fully address it here.[12] But we may observe that the significance of baptism in the life of the church makes it understandable how Christians of different views find it difficult to unite in the same church.

To be sure, some churches seek to accommodate both baptismal practices, effectively making baptism a third-tier issue. While I admire the ecumenical intent of these efforts, I have two practical concerns.

The first concern is *confusion*. Different definitions of baptism lead to different conceptions of the boundaries of the membership of a church, with correspondingly different conceptions of the discipleship of the children within the church. For paedobaptists, the children of believers are considered members of the church from birth, to be treated as "covenant children." Credobaptists understand the ecclesial status of their children differently. In churches where both baptismal practices are adopted, how are the children within the church to be regarded by the rest of the church membership? What is the positive vision set forward by the church for raising children within the context of the church? Presumably, the answer will differ from one child to another based upon the

12. I have addressed the topic of baptism and church membership in Gavin Ortlund, "Can We Reject Paedobaptism and Still Receive Paedobaptists?," Mere Orthodoxy, January 3, 2019, https://mereorthodoxy.com/baptism-church-membership. Jonathan Leeman has offered a thoughtful response, available also at Mere Orthodoxy.

convictions and decisions of the family in question. This seems to send mixed signals to congregants and children, though in situations of exceptional godliness and clear teaching, confusion or disunity can be minimized.[13]

My second concern involves *conscience*. Many denominations that adopt the dual practice of baptism as their official policy often require their ordained and licensed pastors to administer both credobaptism and paedobaptism, in order to enforce this policy consistently from one church to another.[14] This risks violating the consciences of ministers within that denomination who believe there is a normative biblical teaching regarding the proper subjects of baptism. Similarly, efforts at accommodating both baptismal practices within a local church require the current (and future) leadership to be at peace with such a practice, which inevitably excludes some from being able to serve in leadership even as it includes others. Scenarios like this take some of the wind out of the sail of the dual-practice view's appeal to inclusiveness.

I must emphasize, though, that however we navigate our convictions regarding baptism at the ecclesial level, we must not allow this issue to be divisive at the *personal* level. We should go out of our way to show charity toward Christians who hold to a different view than we do, and seek to learn from them. They are part of the body of Christ and, therefore, a part of that people with whom we must have unity in order to make the gospel credible before a watching world (John 17:21). We

13. For example, Immanuel Church in Nashville, the church my father planted, and a church I couldn't regard more highly, does dual practice (as do other prominent churches in the United States, such as College Church in Wheaton, Illinois, and Park Street Church in Boston).

14. The Evangelical Covenant Church, for instance, in its "Policy on Baptism of the Evangelical Covenant Church," stipulates that "since the Covenant recognizes both infant and believer baptism as true baptism it requires all of its ordained and licensed pastors to respect and administer both of these recognized forms of baptism" (https://covchurch.org/wp-content/uploads/sites/2/ . . . /Policy-on-Baptism-churches.pdf, accessed April 4, 2019).

should look for opportunities to link arms and promote the gospel, wherever we can.

Much more needs to be said about baptism, but for the purposes of doing triage, let me stipulate three broad theses within which we will need to carry on further debate and discussion. First, baptism is not a first-rank issue that sets the boundaries of orthodoxy or determines our fruitfulness for the gospel. Rather, sincere and godly Christians can disagree on this topic. Second, baptism is not an unimportant doctrine with no discernable consequence. Rather, it is an issue that bears upon our personal obedience to Christ, the nature and membership of the church, and a robust proclamation of the gospel within the church. Third, we need wisdom and balance to know how to carry our convictions about baptism in a way that honors both the unity of the church and the importance of the issue at hand. Such wisdom will go beyond a blanket evaluation of paedobaptism or credobaptism *as such* and involve a consideration of issues related to the actual practice of baptism in any particular context. These include the ability to distinguish between (1) baptism within Christendom and baptism in a contemporary context in which church and state are separated, (2) covenantal paedobaptism and baptismal regeneration, and (3) *en masse* baptisms for political purposes and principled baptisms for theological purposes.

If you are wrestling with the doctrine of baptism yourself, here are several questions you might find helpful:

1. Is there anything in my heart that takes pride in my view or feels superior to Christians who are on "the other side"? If so, how can I direct my heart back to the gospel as the only source of my identity and "rightness"?
2. Is there anything in me that is disrespectful or dismissive of the importance of this issue? Do I appreciate why

Christians have been willing to die for their differences over this issue? Do I feel superior to, or exasperated with, those Christians who elevate this issue more highly than I do? How can I better understand their concerns and thereby move toward them?

3. Have I taken seriously the urgency of Christ's prayer for the unity of the church (John 17), and am I looking to take whatever steps I can to pursue the realization of this prayer in my own life?
4. What is the right context for me to flourish both in maintaining my own convictions about baptism and in pursuing genuine fellowship and partnership in the gospel with those who differ?

Spiritual Gifts: Continuationism versus Cessationism

Cessationism is the view that certain spiritual gifts mentioned in the New Testament—typically the more miraculous or spectacular gifts such as prophecy, healings, and tongues—have ceased or passed away at some point in antiquity (usually at the closure of the canon or the death of the last apostle). Continuationism, by contrast, affirms the continuation of all spiritual gifts listed in the New Testament throughout the entire church age.

This issue has been important to me ever since my senior year in high school and freshman year in college, when, after a period of great struggle and searching, I became a continuationist in both practice and conviction. Since then, I have observed repeatedly how divisive and polarizing the topic can be, and I look back on some of my own conversations with regret at how I failed to maintain unity as I would have liked.

Here we will survey several different views on spiritual gifts within the Reformed tradition in the effort to situate the topic as a broadly second-rank doctrine (and, in some cases, a third-rank doctrine).

Cessationism is often conceived as the Reformed view, in contrast to Pentecostal and charismatic practice.[15] While many Reformed churches and Christians are cessationist, nothing in Reformed theology absolutely requires this, and historically there is diversity on this question within the Reformed tradition. Cessationism is not endorsed by any major Reformed confessions, and Reformed theologians tend to fall into three broad categories.

First, there are strict cessationists, such as Jonathan Edwards and B. B. Warfield, who deny any genuine manifestations of the miraculous gifts of the Spirit after a certain point in history. These theologians differ, however, on an assortment of questions, such as *which* gifts have ceased (e.g., just revelatory gifts like tongues and prophecy or others such as healing and discerning of spirits?); *when* certain gifts ceased (e.g., at the closure of the canon or the death of the last apostle?); and, most importantly, *why* certain spiritual gifts ceased (e.g., Warfield's argument focuses on the confirmatory role of these gifts in the apostles' ministry, while Edwards's emphasizes the superiority of love to miracles).[16]

Second, some Reformed theologians are soft cessationists, such as John Calvin and John Owen, who maintain that miraculous gifts have ceased in the sense that they are no longer normative for the church, but allow for them at various times and in certain contexts. For example, in the *Institutes*, Calvin conceives of God reviving the offices of apostles, prophets, and evangelists when they are required by the needs of the time:

15. Sinclair Ferguson, "The Reformed View," in *Christian Spirituality: Five Views on Sanctification*, ed. Donald Alexander (Downers Grove, IL: IVP Academic, 1988), 158–61, helpfully outlines a standard Reformed response to Pentecostal theology, operating from a cessationist perspective.

16. See B. B. Warfield, *Counterfeit Miracles* (New York: Charles Scribner's Sons, 1918), and Jonathan Edwards, "The Distinguishing Marks of a Work of the Spirit of God," in *Jonathan Edwards on Revival* (Carlisle, PA: Banner of Truth, 1965), 137–47.

> Those who preside over the government of the Church in accordance with Christ's institution are called by Paul as follows: first apostles, then prophets, thirdly evangelists; fourthly pastors, and finally teachers [Eph. 4:11]. Of these only the two last have an ordinary office in the church; the Lord raised up the first three at the beginning of his Kingdom, *and now and again revives them as the need of the times demands.*[17]

It is evident that Calvin does not conceive of the continuation of the gift of prophecy as a threat to the closure of the canon, as Warfield does. Calvin seems to simply *observe* the absence of this gift rather than require it on theological grounds; he later notes that prophecy "does not exist today *or is less commonly seen.*"[18] Calvin also thinks that God raises up apostles and evangelists in extraordinary times, such as during the Reformation itself—"as has happened in our own day."[19]

Similarly, John Owen, among the greatest of the Puritan theologians, while warning of the superstition and sensationalism of counterfeit miracles, nonetheless allows, "It is not unlikely, but that God might on some occasions for a longer season, put forth his power in some miraculous operations, and so he yet may do, and perhaps doth sometimes."[20] In context, the "operations" to which he refers here are miraculous spiritual gifts. As do the hard cessationists, soft cessationists like Owen and Calvin differ on which gifts ceased, when they did, and why they did.

Third, some Reformed theologians are continuationists, who affirm the validity of miraculous spiritual gifts in some more permanent or normative sense than soft cessationists. Ex-

17. John Calvin, *Institutes of the Christian Religion*, ed. John T. McNeill, trans. Ford Lewis Battles, 2 vols. (Louisville: Westminster John Knox, 2006), 4.3.4, italics mine.

18. Calvin, *Institutes*, 4.3.4, italics mine.

19. Calvin, *Institutes*, 4.3.4.

20. *The Works of John Owen*, ed. Thomas Russell, vol. 4 (London: Paternoster, 1826), 305.

amples of this view would include Martin Luther, John Knox, and Samuel Rutherford. Luther opposed the claims of prophetic gifting by some he regarded as fanatics, and stipulated that there is less need for miraculous attestation to the gospel in regions in which it has already spread. At the same time, he affirmed the continuation of all the gifts. When preaching on the signs mentioned by Jesus in Mark 16, for example, he claimed:

> We must allow these words to remain and not gloss them away, as some have done who said that these signs were manifestations of the Spirit in the beginning of the Christian era and that now they have ceased. That is not right; for the same power is in the church still. And though it is not exercised, that does not matter; we still have the power to do such signs.[21]

Knox (leader of the Reformation in Scotland) and Rutherford (another Scottish minister and framer of the Westminster Confession) were more explicit in affirming specific instances of the gift of prophecy. Rutherford, for example, identified a number of individuals (including Knox himself) "who have foretold things to come even since the ceasing of the Canon of the word," and gave examples of their prophecies, distinguishing this gift of predictive prophecy from inscripturated revelation, which ceased with the closure of the canon.[22]

A similar diversity among Reformed Christians regarding the question of cessationism remains today. There are many

21. Luther, *LW: Sermons*, Lenker edition, 12.190; preached on Ascension Day, 1523, as cited in Douglas A. Oss, "A Pentecostal/Charismatic Response to Robert L. Saucy," in *Are Miraculous Gifts for Today? Four Views*, ed. Wayne A. Grudem, Counterpoints (Grand Rapids, MI: Zondervan, 1996), 167.

22. Samuel Rutherford, *A Survey of the Spirituall Antichrist. Opening the Secrets of Familisme and Antinomianisme in the Antichristian Doctrine of John Saltmarsh (et al.)* (London, 1658), 42, as cited in Oss, "A Pentecostal/Charismatic Response to Robert L. Saucy," 168. Oss offers a helpful summary of Knox and Rutherford throughout his response.

Reformed charismatics, many Reformed cessationists, and many Reformed Christians who are unsure what they think about the gifts. The same holds true for the world of broader evangelicalism.

This survey of the Reformed tradition helps us situate the continuationism-cessationism debate outside the realm of first-rank doctrines. Knox and Warfield differ on the nature of the spiritual gift of prophecy and yet not only have the gospel in common but are relatively close to one another on a theological spectrum.

But where on theological triage *does* this topic rank? Just as we saw with baptism, a larger theological context must be taken into account in order to answer this question. In the first place, among continuationists there are different stances toward the theology of a "second blessing" in which speaking in tongues marks "the initial physical sign" of baptism in the Spirit, an experience that is "distinct from and subsequent to the experience of the new birth."[23] This is the teaching of classic Pentecostalism, but many charismatic Christians, particularly those stemming from the third-wave movement, don't affirm second-blessing theology.[24] Just as the issue of baptismal regeneration adds a layer of complexity to the debate between credobaptists and paedobaptists, so the issue of second-blessing theology adds a layer of complexity to the debate between continuationists and cessationists.

Another layer of complexity is added by the fact that charismatics and noncharismatics often have different views and

23. This language is from points 7 and 8 of the statement of faith of the Assemblies of God, the largest Pentecostal denomination in the world ("Statement of Fundamental Truths," https://ag.org/Beliefs/Statement-of-Fundamental-Truths, accessed March 19, 2019).

24. The third-wave movement refers to the charismatic movement beginning in the 1980s, associated, for example, with Vineyard churches and John Wimber, following on the heels of Pentecostalism in the early twentieth century (the "first wave") and the evangelical charismatic movement of the 1960s and 1970s (the "second wave").

attitudes on a variety of other aspects of Christian spirituality—things like spiritual warfare and demonic possession/oppression, the proper expression of corporate worship, fasting and prayer habits, praying for the sick or the dead, the interpretation of dreams and visions, the measure of optimism in the Christian life, and so forth. These differences are often at play in the discussion of spiritual gifts, even though they are distinct from it.

To see how the practical ramifications of this issue can vary based upon factors like these, consider the following two fictional scenarios.

First, a continuationist named John wants to become a member in a church that is not officially decided on the gifts but is functionally cessationist. John believes that speaking in tongues is valid today, and he practices this gift in his private prayer life. But he believes the implied answer to 1 Corinthians 12:30 ("Do all speak with tongues?") is no, and therefore he does not require that every Christian practice this gift. Moreover, from 1 Corinthians 12:13 he believes that baptism in the Spirit is part of what happens when you become a Christian—it is, as J. I. Packer put it, one part of the "conversion-initiation complex."[25] Therefore, John does not regard speaking in tongues as identifying a distinct spiritual status or level of empowerment for ministry in those who use this gift.

Corresponding to this, while the church is functionally cessationist, they are not disdainful toward charismatic Christians, and they do not regard charismatic practices as destructive or harmful. They are more simply uncertain. During John's membership interview, he shares his conviction on this issue, and the elder performing the interview simply asks John not to be

25. J. I. Packer, *Keep in Step with the Spirit* (Tarrytown, NY: Revell, 1984), 202.

divisive within the body about his conviction. John, having seen in another church how destructive disunity around this issue can be, happily agrees.

Now imagine an alternative scenario. A Christian named Michael is a continuationist who believes that tongues is evidence of baptism in the Holy Spirit, and he has a sincere passion that every Christian would know this blessing. He has only attended Pentecostal churches growing up, but in his interactions with Christians of other traditions, he has observed a dead traditionalism and antiexperiential mentality that he (understandably) regards as "quench[ing] the Spirit" (1 Thess. 5:19). He is wary about this danger and suspicious of Christians who focus on cultivating their knowledge of Scripture without a corresponding concern for practical application and godliness. This understandable and healthy concern sometimes leads him to an anti-intellectual posture, as though theological knowledge itself were dangerous.

Michael attends a church in town that is cessationist—not in an aggressive or mean-spirited way but, nonetheless, as their settled conviction. They have had some unpleasant interactions with a charismatic campus ministry at the university Michael is attending, which have sharpened their views and alerted them to the potential divisiveness of this issue.

It is easy to see from these fictional but not improbable scenarios how the level of importance of the continuationism-cessationism discussion can vary widely based on a range of factors at play. For instance, even supposing that Michael, John, and the leaders of these churches are all equally sincere, godly Christians, these different situations will nonetheless play out differently. Specifically, I would suggest that the situation with John is more like a third-rank issue, and the situation with Michael is more like a second-rank issue.

The primary reason this debate can become a second-rank issue is that cessationism and continuationism are *mutually exclusive* with respect to a church service or Christian gathering. Either such gifts are embraced or they are not. Therefore, what will determine the ranking of continuationism versus cessationism in theological triage involves practical questions such as (1) how important miraculous spiritual gifts are considered to be to the ministry, (2) in what context they are believed to be appropriate (e.g., is exercising them in a church service or in a small group more the ideal?), and (3) what kinds of attitudes and judgments are expressed toward Christians of an opposing view.

In contexts where miraculous spiritual gifts are not centralized, and where different convictions are held with humility and irenicism, this topic can function as a third-rank issue. As with baptism, godliness and clear teaching can reduce divisiveness and thus help an otherwise second-rank issue to function as third rank. For instance, the Acts 29 church-planting network has at times described itself as "charismatic with a seatbelt," and different pastors and leaders within the network take different views. For those who would seek to emulate this approach, the leadership of such ministries will need to work hard to determine what the parameters of their practice are, and to protect the unity of their ministry or church.

In some settings, particularly in light of the complicating factors surveyed above, disagreements about spiritual gifts will necessarily function as second-rank issues. For instance, worshipers convinced from 1 Corinthians 14:1 that prophecy is essential for a healthy church will likely have continual frustration with cessationist churches they attend. Similarly, those convinced that contemporary accounts of tongues are spurious will have a difficult time flourishing in a charismatic church in which speaking in tongues is strongly encouraged.

The most severe strain occurs where the practice of spiritual gifts and demonic deliverance is so heavily emphasized that it becomes the functional "center of gravity" for a particular ministry. This often leads to a displacement of the gospel as the focus of a ministry and an antagonistic relationship with non-charismatic Christians and groups. It is vital for noncharismatics to recognize that when they respond to ministries like this, what they are objecting to is not continuationism per se. Much of what troubles noncharismatics about charismatic practice is not the presence of the gifts but their centralization and abuse.

If you are currently wrestling with this issue, I have one piece of advice. Go above and beyond to show love to Christians who have a different view and to express your own view with humility and grace. Don't underestimate how polarizing this issue can be. This is especially important when you hold to a different view than do the leaders of your church. Be sure to reassure them of your respect for their leadership, and make every effort to "maintain the unity of the Spirit in the bond of peace" (Eph. 4:3). It is tragic when the very gifts the Holy Spirit gives to edify and build up the body of Christ end up tearing us down.

Complementarianism versus Egalitarianism

The debate between complementarians and egalitarians is another example of a second-rank issue. Complementarians affirm distinct roles for men and women in the church and home, while egalitarians affirm the equality of both men and women for various roles in the church and in the marriage relationship. (Now, of course, these definitions and terms are part of what is disputed, and there are other views beyond these two.) Here I'll identify three reasons why this debate is a broadly second-rank issue.

In the first place, we must recognize that, like the debate over spiritual gifts, this debate has a practical dimension: the two positions are mutually exclusive with respect to a local church's governance. Either a church allows only male elders or it allows women to hold office. One often hears people say, "I'm neither egalitarian nor complementarian," seeking to situate themselves in some middle territory. Certainly, we should be open to the nuances involved in different versions of each position, and there are important points of overlap between various options within each camp. But, ultimately, on several of the material points in question, one cannot be in both camps. A church must decide one way or the other whether, for instance, they will ordain female elders. They cannot say both yes and no to this question at the same time.

Moreover, the church bears a responsibility for the discipleship of its married couples and for premarital counseling of members seeking marriage. This will inevitably involve articulating a positive vision of what marriage should be like. Some churches will affirm a role of servant leadership uniquely designed for husbands, patterned after Christ's love for the church. Others will interpret Ephesians 5 as coming in a cultural framework and will emphasize mutual submission within the marriage relationship. Others may opt for a different view, but no one can avoid taking a position. Even if one completely avoids talking about it, that itself is a position.

Second, the complementarian-egalitarian debate is complicated by the larger context of how our culture is currently wrestling with gender and identity. Is gender ultimately a social construct or a predetermined reality? Increasingly, not only is the notion of distinct roles for male and female controversial, but so too is the more basic recognition of masculinity and femininity as stable realities. In this way, different views of gender roles tie into broader visions of human flourishing, such as the proper definition of marriage. Although complementarians and egalitarians often agree that gender complementarity is essential to marriage, the *way* each side does so is based on different presuppositions, and each side often regards the other as conceding either too much or too little to current cultural trends. In other words, complementarianism versus egalitarianism is not simply about how we structure our churches and marriages but also about competing visions of faithfulness to Scripture amid the turbulence of late Western modernity.

A third layer to the complementarian-egalitarian issue involves the biblical hermeneutics of the issue. Disagreements over baptism or spiritual gifts stem from differences on how to interpret Scripture, but the differences usually do not break down along conservative-versus-progressive lines. This is, whether real or perceived, a dynamic involved in the debate over gender roles. The root concern that many complementarians have with egalitarianism is the hermeneutical trajectory it sets, just as egalitarians often regard complementarian hermeneutics as dangerous. Whether these concerns are valid or not, one cannot deny that this is part of the debate, and it escalates its divisiveness.

What all this amounts to is that while the complementarian-egalitarian discussion is not an issue on which the gospel is won or lost, it nonetheless influences in important ways *how* we uphold the gospel. This makes it less surprising when churches or other ministries take a position on it. For instance, the Gospel Coalition, a ministry that seeks to promote gospel-centered ministry for the next generation, affirms complementarianism in its statement of faith.[26] Nonetheless, as a movement of peo-

26. See D. A. Carson and Timothy Keller, eds., *The Gospel as Center: Renewing Our Faith and Reforming Our Ministry Practices* (Wheaton, IL: Crossway, 2012), 274–78.

ple and churches from diverse denominational and theological backgrounds, TGC does not divide over issues like baptism, the millennium, or spiritual gifts.

The Gospel Coalition sometimes faces criticism for affirming complementarianism in its foundation documents but not taking a position on, say, baptism. Isn't it inconsistent to seek to be "gospel-centered" and yet have a position on issues that separate you from others who also love the gospel? Not necessarily. These are decisions of theological triage grounded in the fact that, as we saw in chapter 2, doctrines can be important to the gospel though not essential to it. Therefore, seeking to make the gospel central is not necessarily at odds with affirming the importance of various secondary issues. The TGC Confessional Statement affirms, as parallel examples, double imputation, a propitiating model of the atonement, divine election, and biblical inerrancy—doctrines that are disputed at times by other Christians within the boundaries of orthodoxy.

Consider this analogy: Suppose you are starting an organization that purposes to re-center American legal practice back on the Constitution as the supreme law of the nation. Does this entail that your organization must be neutral on all issues related to constitutional law or subsequent American legal history? Of course not. Any effort to refocus on the center will inevitably engage at least some of the periphery. Similarly, it is false to think that just because an issue is distinct from the gospel, it has no bearing on the gospel. This is at the heart of the recognition of second-rank doctrines as a category.

In light of all this, it is understandable that Christians will at times consider complementarian-egalitarian differences to complicate or perhaps preclude partnership in ministry or in stronger forms of ecclesial alliance. At the same time, we must make several caveats. First, it is important to affirm clearly that this is not a first-rank issue. Complementarians and egalitarians not only can embrace one another as brothers and sisters in Christ who share the gospel, but we should live out the gospel in the way we treat each other. Sadly, this does not always happen. Too often, each side assumes the worst of the other or associates everyone who holds a particular view with its worst representations. Complementarians conceive of egalitarians as compromising liberals, and egalitarians regard complementarians as sexists who oppress women.

It would be better to recognize that there are a variety of expressions of each view and to look for points of contact between the more thoughtful and careful proponents of each side, yet without downplaying the differences. There are godly and intelligent Christians on each side. We must be wary of labeling this a second-rank issue on paper but allowing it to occupy a first-rank position emotionally and practically.

Additionally, we must recognize that not every issue concerning how complementarianism works itself out is second rank. There are all kinds of practical differences within each view. For instance, within the complementarian camp, Andrew Wilson, John Piper, Tom Schreiner, and others recently debated about whether a woman can preach in a local church under the authority of the elders.[27] Questions like this—important as they are—belong in the third-rank category, in my view.

Finally, since I am in the complementarian camp, I will speak to two areas in particular that I believe our tribe needs to be careful about in this discussion.

27. E.g., John Piper, "Can a Woman Preach If Elders Affirm It?," desiringGod, February 16, 2015, http://www.desiringgod.org/interviews/can-a-woman-preach-if-elders-affirm-it; Andrew Wilson, "Women Preachers: A Response to John Piper," Think, May 6, 2015, http://thinktheology.co.uk/blog/article/women_preachers_a_response_to_john_piper; Thomas R. Schreiner, "Why Not to Have a Woman Preach: A Response to Andrew Wilson," desiringGod, May 7, 2015, http://www.desiringgod.org/articles/why-not-to-have-a-woman-preach. Wilson and Jonathan Leeman offered further responses.

First, complementarians need to recognize the complexity inherent in the hermeneutical task of cultural translation from the first century to today. For example, immediately after Paul says, "Wives, submit to your own husbands" (Eph. 5:22), he says, "Bondservants, obey your earthly masters" (Eph. 6:4). We must therefore do more than simply quoting Ephesians 5:22 and then moving on, as though that ended the matter. Similarly, while Paul grounds his prohibition of women teaching men in the church in the doctrine of creation (1 Tim. 2:11–15), he also grounds his teaching on head coverings in the doctrine of creation (1 Cor. 11:2–16). Therefore, the mere appeal to creation does not itself tell us what is a cultural application and what is a transcultural principle.[28]

Don't get me wrong: I am a complementarian and I believe that there are transcultural principles in Ephesians 5 and 1 Timothy 2. But we do not show sufficient respect for this issue or for those with whom we disagree if we act as though the interpretation of these passages were so obvious that any deviation from a complementarian view must be willful compromise. The truth is not so simple, and we should assume the sincerity of those with whom we differ, and should recognize the complexity of applying biblical commandments from one cultural context to another.

Second, complementarians must display sensitivity to the damage done to our sisters in Christ when we are overly restrictive with regard to this view. In some complementarian settings, the spiritual gifts that the Holy Spirit has given to women are tragically undervalued because we ratchet up what is prohibited in Scripture. Our theology of gender roles in the church must not overlook, for instance, the fact that many

28. For a helpful response to egalitarian argumentation on this point, see Craig Blomberg, "A Response to Craig Keener," in *Two Views on Women in Ministry*, rev. ed., ed. James R. Beck, Counterpoints (Grand Rapids, MI: Zondervan, 2005), 251.

women throughout the Old Testament were prophets (Miriam, Deborah, Huldah, et al.), and that in the New Testament the gift of prophecy is clearly given to both men and women (Acts 2:17–18; 21:9; 1 Cor. 11:5).

In addition, a strong case can be made that women served as deacons in the New Testament. While the word *diakonos* can be used in a nontechnical sense to mean "servant," the fact that "our sister Phoebe" is called a "[*diakonos*] of the church at Cenchreae" (Rom. 16:1) makes it much more natural to take the term as referring to the official position of the church. Additionally, it seems more plausible that the "women" of 1 Timothy 3:11 are deaconesses rather than the wives of deacons, since it would be perplexing for Paul to list requirements for the wives of deacons but not for elders. It is also striking that the church had deaconesses at various points in her history (e.g., throughout the first few centuries, in Calvin's Geneva), despite generally operating in far more patriarchal cultures than ours.[29]

Complementarians should humbly consider where we have at times gone too far. Our posture toward this topic should not show greater fear of affirming what is forbidden than of forbidding what is affirmed. We must celebrate the contribution that every member can make to the body of Christ.[30]

If you are interested in exploring this issue further, let me mention two helpful resources:

Keller, Timothy, with Kathy Keller. "Singleness and Marriage." In *The Meaning of Marriage: Facing the Com-*

29. For a fuller treatment of this issue, see Thomas Schreiner, "Does the Bible Support Female Deacons? Yes," The Gospel Coalition, February 19, 2019, https://www.thegospelcoalition.org/article/bible-support-female-deacons-yes/.

30. I develop this concern more fully in my article "4 Dangers for Complementarians," The Gospel Coalition, November 14, 2014, https://www.thegospelcoalition.org/article/four-dangers-for-complementarians.

plexities of Commitment with the Wisdom of God, 192–218. New York: Dutton, 2011.

Köstenberger, Andreas J., and Margaret Elizabeth Köstenberger. *God's Design for Man and Woman: A Biblical-Theological Survey.* Wheaton, IL: Crossway, 2014.

The Need for Wisdom

As I warned, my treatment of each of these issues has been brief. I have not tried to resolve them. Hopefully, however, this discussion has drawn attention to several factors that complicate judgments of theological triage. Whether an issue is a second-rank or third-rank doctrine, or how important it is as a second-rank doctrine, often depends on what other doctrines come along with it and the attitude with which it is held. We have to take into account the "whole package" for its real-life consequence.

Many of us don't like to live with ambiguity. We like to have things nailed down. We want to know, once for all, what number to assign to each particular issue so that we can function in light of that judgment.

Unfortunately, real life is more complicated than neat categories allow. Many doctrines defy a once-for-all classification without consideration of context. So, just as courage is the great need surrounding first-rank doctrines, the great need surrounding second-rank doctrines is wisdom. Theological triage is not a matter of crunching the numbers. It is not a math equation. There are practical and relational nuances constantly in play.

Therefore, among the most important practices for doing theological triage effectively are prayer and humble reliance upon the Holy Spirit. Theological wisdom, like all forms of wisdom, is more a spiritual matter than an intellectual one.

In this area of life, as in every other, we must heed the advice of Solomon:

> do not lean on your own understanding. . . .
> Be not wise in your own eyes. (Prov. 3:5, 7)

Realizing our need for wisdom may seem like a small gain, but it encourages us to humbly ask God to supply what we lack. Happily, this is a prayer he has promised to answer (James 1:5).

6

Why We Should Not Divide over Tertiary Doctrines

In both war and theology, there are battles to avoid. Just as we can be ineffective because of compromise or inertia, so too we can be ineffective because of impulsiveness or haste. In fact, I would suggest that a wise theologian, like a wise military general, will be characterized by patience far more frequently than by action. Most of the battles you *could* fight, you shouldn't. And I'd go so far as to say that the majority of doctrinal fights Christians have today tend to be over third-rank issues—or fourth. We deeply need to cultivate greater doctrinal forbearance, composure, and resilience.[1]

In this chapter I'll propose two doctrinal disputes as examples of this need: the creation days of Genesis 1 and the nature of the millennium in Revelation 20. Christians often divide

1. On March 26, 2019, my friend Jonathan Leeman tweeted a comment a pastor put to him: "I thought my job as a pastor would focus on getting my church members to encourage one another to do what the Bible commands. Instead, most of my job is keeping my church members from demanding things of each other the Bible never does."

from one another over how to interpret these passages at the beginning and end of the Bible. This chapter suggests that we should not divide, at any level, over these two issues.

This is not to say that *everything* related to protology (first things) and eschatology (last things) is third rank. These areas contain a variety of first-rank doctrines, such as creation ex nihilo (from nothing) or the bodily nature of Christ's second coming.

But it is a historical irony that American evangelicals have tended to divide over the peripheral aspects of creation and eschatology while ignoring the more central aspects of these doctrines. Thus, many evangelicals focus more on the timing of the rapture, the identity of the anti-Christ, and the nature of the millennium (all, in my view, third-rank doctrines) than they do on the second coming of Christ, the final resurrection, or the final judgment (all, in my view, first-rank doctrines). Similarly, many evangelicals are intimately familiar with the "creation wars" but have never given any sustained reflection to more basic questions about the goodness and contingency of creation, on which the early church expended so much energy, and which are vital to a Christian worldview.

Fighting over tertiary issues is unhelpful. But fighting over tertiary issues while simultaneously neglecting primary issues is even worse. So here we will engage these two issues to illustrate where we can benefit from critical reflection on our doctrinal priorities.

Why Christians Shouldn't Divide over the Millennium

We begin at the end. The millennium of Revelation 20 has been a divisive issue in recent church history.[2] In particular, pre-

2. The debate simply turns on the timing of Christ's return in relation to the thousand-year golden era prophesied by John in Revelation 20:1–6. I defined each of the major views in chapter 3.

millennialism stood alongside biblical inerrancy as an identity issue in the early fundamentalist-evangelical movement. In his autobiography, for instance, the evangelical leader Carl F. H. Henry describes several occasions on which it was a point of division among early fundamentalists and evangelicals.[3]

Or consider the early years of Fuller Theological Seminary, when the institution was thoroughly premillennial; the millennium was in the seminary's statement of faith, and the faculty was sharply divided over a pre-tribulation versus a post-tribulation view of the rapture. George Marsden calls this a "leading issue," with Harold Lindsell, Wilbur Smith, Gleason Archer, Carl Henry, Everett Harrison, and Charles Woodbridge lining up for the pre-trib view versus George Eldon Ladd, Edward John Carnell, Clarence Roddy, and Daniel Fuller on the post-trib side.[4] In that setting, Ladd's *The Blessed Hope* (1956), a case for historical premillennialism, was considered controversial. Imagine how amillennialism or postmillennialism would have been viewed!

The scene is different today. Many denominations and churches have loosened their requirements on this issue and allow for a variety of views. David Roach notes, "In the mid-twentieth century, Memphis pastor R. G. Lee quipped that he wouldn't even say 'ahh' at the dentist, a reference to the strong aversion he and other theological conservatives in the Southern Baptist Convention felt toward Amillennialism."[5] A greater diversity of views exists among Southern Baptists today,[6] as well

3. Carl F. H. Henry, *Confessions of a Theologian: An Autobiography* (Waco, TX: Word, 1986), 67, 149.

4. George Marsden, *Reforming Fundamentalism: Fuller Seminary and the New Evangelicalism* (Grand Rapids, MI: Eerdmans, 1995), 151.

5. David Roach, "Southern Baptists and the Millennium," *SBC Life* 22, no. 5 (June 2014); available online June 1, 2014, http://www.sbclife.net/article/2295/southern-baptists-and-the-millennium.

6. The Baptist Faith and Message simply affirms that "Jesus Christ will return personally and visibly in glory to the earth" (art. 10).

as among other denominations, some of which are changing their positions.[7]

At the same time, many churches, networks, and denominations still mandate premillennialism. Tom Schreiner notes, "For some, premillennialism is virtually equivalent to orthodoxy."[8] Robert Clouse calls the debate "one of the most divisive elements in recent Christian history."[9]

I think the role that the millennium has played in dividing evangelicals is unfortunate. Here I offer three reasons why I think we should not divide, in any context, over differences regarding the millennium—a biblical, practical, and historical argument.

First, biblically, the millennium is explicitly taught in only one passage, and it is a notoriously difficult passage to interpret, coming in perhaps the most difficult book of the New Testament. This distinguishes the millennium from doctrines that result from the convergence of biblical claims or the development of a particular theme or motif throughout the Bible. Of course, premillennialists claim that the millennium is suggested or implied in other parts of the Bible, and all millennial views involve argumentation from a combination of texts and considerations. But it seems difficult to deny that the primary passage at play—the only one that actually mentions a millennium—is Revelation 20:1–6. It is questionable whether premillennialism would exist if Revelation 20 did not.

---

7. For instance, the Evangelical Free Church of America is considering a motion to amend article 9 of its Statement of Faith by removing the word "premillennial" and replacing it with "glorious." You can read the denomination's helpful articulation of its reasons for this proposed change in its "Proposal to Amend EFCA Statement of Faith: A Rationale for the Change," EFCA, https://www.efca.org/resources/document/proposal-amend-efca-statement-faith, accessed April 7, 2019.

8. Thomas R. Schreiner, endorsement of Sam Storms, *Kingdom Come: The Amillennial Alternative* (Fearn, Ross-shire, UK: Mentor, 2013).

9. Robert G. Clouse, postscript to *The Meaning of the Millennium: Four Views*, ed. Robert G. Clouse (Downers Grove, IL: InterVarsity Press, 1977), 209.

This certainly does not, in itself, disqualify premillennialism (or any other view, for that matter). There are other doctrines we believe on the basis of relatively few texts (such as the virgin birth, which I have here defended as first rank!). Moreover, even one text is enough to require our assent, should we become convinced in our understanding of it. But as I have said, the passage that explicitly speaks of a millennium is located in one of the most difficult books in the entire Bible. Revelation is filled with apocalyptic imagery and symbolism that is notoriously challenging to interpret, and Revelation 20:1–6 is no exception. Even allowing for the premillennialist's appeal to the notion of progressive revelation,[10] we should be cautious about dividing from other Christians over a view based primarily on one highly disputed text, on which even seasoned theologians like Saint Augustine change their view (more on Augustine in a moment).

Second, practically, the doctrine of the millennium makes significantly less practical difference to the Christian life and church health than do the second-rank doctrines we have surveyed. Now, of course, some Christians dispute this claim. Most commonly, the objection arises from within the premillennialist camp in relation to the feared hermeneutical implications of amillennialism and postmillennialism. If we "spiritualize" this passage, what others will follow? As John Walvoord expressed this concern, "The modernist who spiritualizes the resurrection of Christ does so by almost the same techniques as are used by B. B. Warfield

10. Wayne Grudem, *Systematic Theology: An Introduction to Biblical Doctrine* (Grand Rapids, MI: Zondervan, 1994), 1117, argues that this is similar to the situation at the end of the Old Testament era: "The entire Old Testament has no explicit teaching to the effect that the Messiah would come twice, once as a suffering Messiah who would die and rise again, earning our salvation, and then later as a conquering King to rule over the earth." For many, however, a millennial interlude subsequent to the return of Christ would seem a greater surprise than two distinct messianic comings. After all, amillennialists and postmillennialists argue that the New Testament *is* explicit that the resurrection of the dead is occasioned by the second coming of Christ: "For as in Adam all die, so also in Christ shall all be made alive. But each in his own order: Christ the firstfruits, then *at his coming* those who belong to Christ" (1 Cor. 15:22–23).

who finds heaven described in Revelation 20:1–10."[11] As George Ladd points out, however, there is a crucial difference between the liberal who acknowledges that the resurrection of Christ is taught in the Bible but rejects it on other grounds and the amillennialist who accepts a heavenly picture in Revelation precisely because he thinks that is what the text means. Even if both the liberal and the amillennialist are wrong, they are wrong for different reasons and in different ways. Ladd therefore replies that the millennium "is a question where equally evangelical scholars who accept the Bible as the inspired Word of God should be able to disagree without the accusation 'liberal.'"[12] Moreover, even if we granted that the interpretative difference between premillennialism and the alternatives consists of a "loosening," why not divide over this hermeneutic itself, rather than its application in this instance?

Some might protest that the millennium is important because it significantly affects our outlook on the future, and related to this, our posture toward the current culture. However, much of the pessimism or optimism that has historically been associated with views of the millennium is not intrinsic to the position in question. For instance, some amillennialists have been very pessimistic about the future, but others are not; and there is nothing in amillennialism that *requires* cultural pessimism (I myself am a cheerful amillennialist). To a lesser extent, this appears to be true of the other views, though some argue that optimism is an essential feature of postmillennialism.[13] Thus, even if we conclude that our outlook on the future is a significant factor in the Christian life (itself not an obvious

11. John F. Walvoord, *The Millennial Kingdom* (Findlay, OH: Dunham, 1959), 71.
12. George Eldon Ladd, "Historic Premillennialism," in Clouse, *Meaning of the Millennium*, 20.
13. Greg Bahnsen, "The *Prima Facie* Acceptability of Postmillennialism," *The Journal of Christian Reconstruction* 3, no. 2 (1976–1977): 65.

point), it would be better to address this issue of our future expectation directly, rather than views on the millennium that are taken to influence that expectation. This is a great need in the millennium debate—to disentangle the actual views from the cultural attitudes that have been associated with them but are not strictly necessary to them.[14]

A third reason not to divide over millennial views concerns the church's historical stance on this issue. Sometimes church history can help us identify where our theological bandwidth differs from that of other Christians. That is the case with the millennium. Specifically, the default American evangelical posture toward premillennialism is somewhat eccentric when seen against the backdrop of the global and historical church.

Throughout church history, the notion of a literal thousand-year reign on earth after Christ's coming has often been called "chiliasm" and "millenarianism." A rough version of this view was held by some early church fathers, such as Justin Martyr and Irenaeus, and it occasionally cropped up with a more apocalyptic emphasis among certain separatist groups in the early and medieval church.[15] However, contrary to the claims of some, chiliasm was not the universal view among the pre-Augustinian church fathers, and it was not the earliest common view but rather came into bloom in the second century.[16] Moreover, from the time of Augustine's change of mind in favor of amillennialism in *The City of God* in the early fifth century up

14. As Samuel Allen Dawson notes, "The danger of discussing these issues on an attitudinal level—pessimistic or optimistic—is that such a discussion may lead to the choosing of a doctrine for reasons other than Scripture" ("The Millennium: An Examination and Analysis of the Methodologies and Strategies of the Various Positions on the Millennial Issue" [PhD diss., Trinity Evangelical Divinity School, 1998], 8).

15. Michael Horton, *The Christian Faith: A Systematic Theology for Pilgrims on the Way* (Grand Rapids, MI: Zondervan, 2011), 923, 925, notes the presence of apocalyptic forms of millenarianism among the Montanists in the early church and various medieval sects like the Albigensians and Cathari.

16. For a helpful overview, see Charles E. Hill, Regnum Caelorum*: Patterns of Millennial Thought in Early Christianity*, 2nd ed. (Grand Rapids, MI: Eerdmans, 2001).

through the seventeenth century, all such premillennial schemas were eclipsed by a widespread expectation that Christ's millennial reign would precede his return.[17] The prevailing view during this time is well expressed by Thomas Aquinas, who argued that the thousand years of Revelation 20 refers to

> the whole time of the Church in which the martyrs as well as other saints reign with Christ, both in the present Church which is called the kingdom of God, and also—as far as souls are concerned—in the heavenly country; for "the thousand" means perfection.[18]

This view broadly held sway among the Reformers and throughout the subsequent Reformed tradition.

Thus, premillennialism has been the minority view for most of church history, and dispensational premillennialism—the default view of the end times in many evangelical circles—did not even exist until the nineteenth century.[19] Not only this, but premillennialism has often been a highly controversial view. Louis Berkhof claims that "the doctrine of the millennium has never yet been embodied in a single Confession, and therefore cannot be regarded as a dogma of the Church."[20] Yet, if any millennial view *has* had a precarious relationship with orthodoxy, it is premillennialism. For instance, it was condemned as superstition by the Council of Ephesus in 431,[21] and some

---

17. For further summary, see Gregg R. Allison, *Historical Theology: An Introduction to Christian Doctrine* (Grand Rapids, MI: Zondervan, 2011), 683–701.

18. Thomas Aquinas, *Summa contra Gentiles*, 5 vols. (Garden City, NY: Doubleday, 1955–1957), 4:329, quoted in Thomas C. Oden, *Classic Christianity: A Systematic Theology* (New York: HarperOne, 1992), 806.

19. For a helpful overview of dispensational premillennialism, both in its historical development and in understanding how it has become so popular among American evangelicals, see Storms, *Kingdom Come*, 43–69.

20. Louis Berkhof, *The History of Christian Doctrine* (Grand Rapids, MI: Baker, 1975), 264.

21. See the discussion in Stanley J. Grenz, *The Millennial Maze: Sorting Out Evangelical Options* (Downers Grove, IL: InterVarsity Press, 1992), 44; cf. Michael J. Svigel, "The Phantom Heresy: Did the Council of Ephesus (431) Condemn Chiliasm?," Bible.org,

later Reformed confessions extended this judgment. The First Helvetic Confession, for instance, states, "We also reject the Jewish dream of a millennium, or golden age on earth, before the last judgment" (art. 11).

There should be caution in evaluating some of the condemnations of "chiliasm" and "millenarianism" we find throughout church history, since what was being rejected at times differed significantly from modern evangelical premillennialism. In the early church, millenarian views were originally associated with the Montanists, named after Montanus, who claimed special revelation indicating that Christ would return within his lifetime. Similarly, when John Calvin condemned the "chiliasts" in his day because "their fiction is too childish either to need or to be worth a refutation," he appears to have envisioned a more fanatical view among the Anabaptists that he regarded as endangering the eternality of heaven.[22] In other words, the premillennialism that has stirred controversy throughout church history has often done so because of its association with fanatical and/or heretical adherents. We must also bear in mind that the kinds of postmillennialism and amillennialism one finds throughout church history at times differ from modern expressions of these views. For instance, Augustine understood reigning with Christ in Revelation 20 to involve *both* the ruling of deceased believers in heaven during the church age *and* the spiritual and ecclesiastical reign of believers on earth during the church age.[23]

September 17, 2004, https://bible.org/article/phantom-heresy-did-council-ephesus-431-condemn-chiliasm#P8_513.

22. John Calvin, *Institutes of the Christian Religion*, ed. John T. McNeill, trans. Ford Lewis Battles, 2 vols. (Louisville: Westminster John Knox, 2006), 3.25.5. Calvin's lack of attention to the millennium is striking; he devotes the bulk of his treatment of eschatology in the *Institutes* to the final resurrection.

23. As noted, for instance, by Anthony A. Hoekema, *The Bible and the Future* (Grand Rapids, MI: Eerdmans, 1979), 183.

But if the church's historical testimony should not be used to label premillennialism a heresy, it should, at least, discourage us from elevating it as a litmus test of orthodoxy. For instance, it is difficult to sustain the claim that amillennialism or postmillennialism reflects a liberal or aberrant posture toward Scripture, since it would require us to regard as hermeneutically suspect essentially the entire church for twelve centuries—including Augustine and the medieval church, John Calvin and the other Reformers, and John Owen and virtually all the Puritans. Alternatively, if someone claims that modern voices are more relevant than premodern voices for testing our hermeneutics on this question, we must reckon with the towering fact that the staunchest defender of a conservative doctrine of Scripture in the modern era, B. B. Warfield, was a postmillennialist, as were most of his colleagues at Princeton Theological Seminary at the time. It puts one in a rather awkward position, to say the least, to suggest that the hermeneutics of John Calvin, Jonathan Edwards, and B. B. Warfield are in danger of setting us on the slippery slope toward liberalism.

Earlier I quoted J. Gresham Machen's *Christianity and Liberalism* on the nature of the sacraments. In the same context, he treats the millennium, stating that premillennialism caused him "serious concern," since it is coupled with "a false method of interpreting Scripture which in the long run will be productive of harm." At the same time, Machen emphasizes how much he has in common with those who hold this view, and he expresses his unwillingness to divide from them:

> Yet how great is our agreement with those who hold the premillennial view! They share to the full our reverence for the authority of the Bible, and differ from us only in the interpretation of the Bible; they share ascription of deity to

the Lord Jesus, and our supernaturalistic conception both of the entrance of Jesus into the world and of the consummation when He shall come again. Certainly, then, from our point of view, their error, serious though it may be, is not deadly error; and Christian fellowship, with loyalty not only to the Bible but to the great creeds of the Church, can still unite us to them.[24]

Machen was the leader of the great conservative split from the mainline Presbyterian church in the early twentieth century. He can hardly be accused of being weak on sound doctrine or unsympathetic to the cause of theological polemics. We would do well to consider his appeal that "Christian fellowship" need not be at stake in disagreements over this issue.

The diversity of millennial views in the church today should also induce humility and carefulness in our judgments. Many teachers in the church, including conservative teachers who cannot be accused of doctrinal minimalism, avoid even taking a position on the millennium. For instance, R. C. Sproul's book on eschatology concludes with a chapter on the millennium in which he simply describes the different views and refrains from taking a position.[25] Other pastors go further in the interest of unity. Mark Dever, senior pastor of Capitol Hill Baptist Church in Washington, DC, has put a great deal of thought into how local churches should function, as have his colleagues at 9Marks. In 2009, he made a strong appeal that churches need not divide over the millennium:

What you believe about the millennium—how you interpret these thousand years—is not something that it is necessary for us to agree upon in order to have a

24. J. Gresham Machen, *Christianity and Liberalism* (New York: Macmillan, 1923), 49.

25. R. C. Sproul, *The Last Days according to Jesus: When Did Jesus Say He Would Return?* (Grand Rapids, MI: Baker, 1998), 193–203.

> congregation together. The Lord Jesus Christ prayed in John 17:21 that we Christians might be one. Of course all true Christians are one in that we have his Spirit, we share his Spirit, we desire to live out that unity. But that unity is supposed to be evident as a testimony to the world around us. . . . So if you're a pastor and you're listening to me, you understand me correctly if you think I'm saying you are in sin if you lead your congregation to have a statement of faith that requires a particular millennial view. I do not understand why that has to be a matter of uniformity in order to have Christian unity in a local congregation.[26]

Supposing that this appeal is right and that churches should not divide over the millennium—this does not entail, of course, that the millennium is unimportant. God has inspired Revelation 20:1–6 for our edification, and it is our responsibility to study and apply this passage to the best of our ability. The point is that we can debate our differences from *within* the context of Christian unity, expressed in local church membership or any other context. In 2009, John Piper modeled this kind of earnest dialogue by hosting a discussion about the millennium with a representative of each view present.[27] It was edifying to see how all the spokesmen involved cared passionately about the correct interpretation of Scripture and yet were able to debate their differences with a discernable spirit of brotherhood in the gospel.

---

26. The text of this sermon is posted by Justin Taylor, "Dever: 'You Are in Sin If You Lead Your Congregation to Have a Statement of Faith That Requires a Particular Millennial View,'" The Gospel Coalition, July 14, 2009, https://www.thegospelcoalition.org/blogs/justin-taylor/dever-you-are-in-sin-if-you-lead-your.

27. The participants were Jim Hamilton (professor of New Testament at Southern Baptist Theological Seminary), Sam Storms (pastor of Bridgeway Church, Oklahoma City), and Doug Wilson (pastor of Christ Church, Moscow, Idaho). The debate, titled "An Evening of Eschatology," September 27, 2009, can be viewed at https://www.desiringgod.org/interviews/an-evening-of-eschatology.

Why Christians Shouldn't Divide over the Creation Days

Now back to the beginning. One of the most controversial issues in the church today, at least in my context in the United States, concerns the interpretation of the days of creation in Genesis 1. A Christian radio host once told me that there were three topics the station knew would get calls when addressed in a broadcast, no matter the perspective offered: racism, Donald Trump, and creation.

Al Mohler, who has been instrumental in popularizing the notion of "theological triage," is an outspoken proponent of a young-earth-creation view. Nonetheless, Mohler identifies the debate over the creation days as a third-rank doctrine, stating that not only does he have many friends who hold to a contrary position, but he hires them as faculty.[28] Let me offer a few brief remarks in agreement with Mohler's ranking of this debate.

Like the millennial debate, different views on Genesis 1 are less practically relevant to the organization of a local church or its worship, evangelism, and witness to the gospel than a number of other doctrines are. Some young-earth creationists dispute this claim, of course. Some even argue that interpreting the days of Genesis 1 as something other than twenty-four-hour days undermines the gospel itself, effectively making this issue a first-rank doctrine. Some argue that if we "compromise" on a literal reading of the first chapter of the Bible, why won't we compromise elsewhere? Others claim that allowing for animal death prior to the human fall makes God the

28. This comment was made during a discussion with C. John Collins on the question "Does Scripture Speak Definitively to the Age of the Universe?," held at Trinity Evangelical Divinity School in February 2017. See http://henrycenter.tiu.edu/resource/genesis-the-age-of-the-earth-does-scripture-speak-definitively-on-the-age-of-the-universe.

author of evil. Proponents of this view are quite outspoken, and it has become widely embraced in many American evangelical churches.

On both of these points, history can once again provide valuable perspective. The creation days have not always been so divisive, even since Darwin. In evangelical circles, particularly American evangelical circles since the 1960s, the creation debate has developed in a somewhat eccentric, parochial way.

For instance, many conservative Protestants in the nineteenth and early twentieth centuries had no hesitation seeking to reconcile Genesis 1 with geological data indicating an older earth and older universe. Many prominent critics of theological liberalism, such as Machen, and defenders of an orthodox view of Scripture, such as Warfield, affirmed an older earth and an older universe and had no trouble reconciling this with Genesis 1. The same can be said of an enormous variety of Christian leaders representing diverse places and traditions, from the Baptist preacher Charles Spurgeon, to the Scottish churchman Thomas Chalmers, to the Reformed Dutch theologian Herman Bavinck, to evangelical leaders like Carl Henry in the United States or John Stott in Britain—and on and on we could go.[29]

Take Charles Spurgeon as an example. In a sermon on the Holy Spirit, preached on June 17, 1855, four years prior to the publication of Darwin's *On the Origin of Species*, Spurgeon quoted Genesis 1:2 and then claimed:

> We do not know how remote the period of the creation of this globe may be—certainly many millions of years before the time of Adam. Our planet has passed through various stages of existence, and different kinds of crea-

29. For further reading, see Ronald L. Numbers, *The Creationists: From Scientific Creationism to Intelligent Design*, 2nd ed. (Cambridge, MA: Harvard University Press, 2006), and *Darwin, Creation, and the Fall: Theological Challenges*, ed. R. J. Berry and T. A. Noble (Nottingham, UK: Apollos, 2009).

> tures have lived on its surface, all of which have been fashioned by God.[30]

Spurgeon proceeded to describe the Spirit's role in bringing order out of chaos in the process of creation, quoting a John Milton poem to highlight the Spirit's power in this role. In a sermon a few months later, he claimed,

> We have discovered that thousands of years before that God was preparing chaotic matter to make it a fit abode for man, putting races of creatures upon it who might die and leave behind the marks of His handiwork and marvelous skill before He tried His hand on man.[31]

What is most striking, perhaps, is not so much Spurgeon's affirmation of millions of years before Adam but his apparent lack of anxiety or difficulty in accepting this notion without much argumentation or concern in the context of a sermon.

Things have changed since Spurgeon's day. Views on creation have grown more polarized as the creation-evolution debate has become a more publicly visible flashpoint in American culture through events such as the Scopes trial in the 1920s, and particularly since the launching of the "young-earth creationist" movement in 1961 with the publication of John Whitcomb and Henry Morris's *The Genesis Flood*.[32] Prior to this, young-earth creationism was not insisted on by most Christians or widely perceived as the conservative or default Christian view. The Scofield Reference Bible (enormously popular in the early twentieth century) had advocated for the gap theory, a species of

30. Charles Spurgeon, sermon 30, "The Power of the Holy Ghost," in *The Complete Works of C. H. Spurgeon*, vol. 1, *Sermons 1 to 53* (Cleveland, OH: Pilgrim, 2013), 88.

31. Charles Spurgeon, sermons 41–42, "Unconditional Election," in *The Complete Works of C. H. Spurgeon*, 1:122.

32. John C. Whitcomb and Henry M. Morris, *The Genesis Flood: The Biblical Record and Its Scientific Implications* (Philadelphia: Presbyterian and Reformed, 1961).

old-earth creationism. William Jennings Bryan (who represented the prosecution at the Scopes trial) held to a day-age view; this too is an old-earth creationist interpretation of Genesis 1.[33] Such views were common enough that, strikingly, the conservative evangelical publisher Moody Press could even decline to publish *The Genesis Flood* out of concern that "firm insistence on six literal days could offend their constituency."[34] As Tim Keller summarizes:

> Despite widespread impression to the contrary, both inside and outside the church, modern Creation Science was not the traditional response of conservative and evangelical Protestants in the nineteenth century when Darwin's theory first became known. . . . R. A. Torrey, the fundamentalist editor of *The Fundamentals* (published from 1910–1915, which gave definition to the term "fundamentalist"), said that it was possible "to believe thoroughly in the infallibility of the Bible and still be an evolutionist of a certain type. . . ." The man who defined the doctrine of Biblical inerrancy, B. B. Warfield of Princeton (d. 1921) believed that God may have used something like evolution to bring about life-forms.[35]

Additionally, it is not just in the modern era that Christians have read Genesis 1 differently. Many in the early church, far before any pressure from scientific discovery of the age of the universe, held that the days of Genesis 1 were not twenty-four-hour periods. Saint Augustine, for example, in the fourth and

---

33. The gap theory, popularized by Thomas Chalmers in the nineteenth century, affirms a gap between Genesis 1:1 and 1:2, while the day-age view sees the "days" as long epochs of time.

34. Matthew Barrett and Ardel B. Caneday, introduction to *Four Views on the Historical Adam*, ed. Matthew Barrett and Ardel B. Caneday, Counterpoints (Grand Rapids, MI: Zondervan, 2013), 19.

35. Tim Keller, *The Reason for God: Belief in an Age of Skepticism* (New York: Dutton, 2008), 262n18.

fifth centuries, wrote several different commentaries on Genesis. In his final effort, a "literal" commentary on Genesis, he emphasized the difficulty of this question: "It is indeed an arduous and extremely difficult task for us to get through to what the writer meant with these six days, however concentrated our attention and lively our minds."[36]

Augustine's struggle with Genesis 1 stands contrary to those who claim that the interpretation of the text is a matter of obviousness or common sense. Ultimately, concerning the relation of twenty-four-hour days as we know them to the "days" of Genesis 1, Augustine affirmed that "we must be in no doubt that they are not at all like them, but very, very dissimilar."[37] Augustine understood the depiction of God's work of creation in seven days as an accommodation to human understanding, drawing a comparison between divine creation and a human week of work. Augustine came to this view for a variety of textual reasons, including the problem of light coming in day 1 prior to the luminaries in day 4, the problem of dischronology introduced in Genesis 2:4–6, and the presentation of God's rest on day 7.[38]

Early Christians also held different intuitions about animal death than are common today. Responding to the criticisms of God's creation by the Manichaeans, Augustine vigorously defended the goodness of animal and plant death before the fall:

> It is ridiculous to condemn the faults of beasts and of trees, and other such mortal and mutable things as are void of

36. Augustine, *On Genesis: A Refutation of the Manichees, . . . The Literal Meaning of Genesis*, trans. Edmund Hill, ed. John E. Rotelle (Hyde Park, NY: New City, 2002), 241.

37. Augustine, *Literal Meaning of Genesis*, 267.

38. I unpack Augustine's views further in Gavin Ortlund, *Retrieving Augustine's Doctrine of Creation: Ancient Wisdom for Current Controversy* (Downers Grove, IL: IVP Academic, 2020).

> intelligence, sensation, or life, even though these faults should destroy their corruptible nature; for these creatures received, at their Creator's will, an existence fitting them.[39]

Both Ambrose and Basil, in their famous treatment of the creation days, emphasized God's wisdom in creating carnivorous animals. Basil, for instance, warned against rash judgments about how God created the animal kingdom:

> Let nobody accuse the Creator of having produced venomous animals, destroyers and enemies of our life. Else let them consider it a crime in the schoolmaster when he disciplines the restlessness of youth by the use of the rod and whip to maintain order.[40]

In the medieval period, Thomas Aquinas maintained that "the nature of animals was not changed by man's sin, as if those whose nature now it is to devour the flesh of others, would then have lived on herbs, like the lion and falcon."[41]

This historical backdrop provides context for our current debates about creation. It also helps us to appreciate that many of those who affirm a "historical" reading of Genesis 1 do not interpret the days as twenty-four hours. The issue is not *whether* but *how* Genesis 1 is narrating history. Virtually all commentators recognize differences of language and style between Genesis 1:1–2:3 and the rest of Genesis, as well as between the more compressed, pictorial narrative of Genesis 1–11 and the subsequent narrative of Genesis 12–50.[42] The Bible uses

39. Augustine, *The City of God* 12.4, trans. Marcus Dods (New York: Modern Library, 2000), 383.

40. Basil, *Hexaemeron* 9.5, in Basil, *Letters and Selected Works*, vol. 8 of *Nicene and Post-Nicene Fathers*, ed. Philip Schaff and Henry Wace, trans. Blomfield Jackson (Peabody, MA: Hendrickson, 1994), 105.

41. Thomas Aquinas, *Summa theologica*, I, q. 96, art. 1, trans. Fathers of the English Dominican Province (Notre Dame, IN: Christian Classics, 1948), 486.

42. For an eloquent expression of this point, see J. I. Packer, "Hermeneutics and Genesis 1–11," *Southwestern Journal of Theology* 44, no. 1 (2001).

diverse literary genres to convey historical events, and many historical passages employ stylized, symbolical, or elevated language. David's poetic descriptions of salvation in Psalm 18, the night visions of Zechariah 1–6, Deborah and Barak's song in Judges 5, and John's apocalyptic visions in Revelation are all concerned with events that happen in history. But it would be hermeneutically careless to read these passages in the same way we read, say, the Gospels, which are widely considered in the genre of ancient biography. We should work hard to identify and understand the literary character of each passage in which the Bible narrates historical events, including Genesis 1.[43]

Much more needs to be said about the creation debate, but hopefully what is said here will at least encourage more humility and openness in the process. Think of it like this: if you accept only twenty-four-hour-day interpretations of Genesis 1 within your church or theological circle, then the following Christians become unacceptable to you: Augustine, Charles Spurgeon, B. B. Warfield, and Carl Henry. Does this seem right? This is exactly the kind of situation in which theological triage would urge caution.

We can happily coexist within the church amid differences on this issue. Our unity in the gospel is not at stake. Instead, we should put more focus on the aspects of the doctrine of creation that Christians have classically emphasized and that are distinctive to a broadly Judeo-Christian worldview, such as creation ex nihilo, the historicity of the fall, and the fact that human beings are made in God's image. These are better hills to die on.

Being Strong Enough Not to Fight

One of my friends is taking Tae Kwon Do lessons with his son. Explaining why he is grateful for what his son is learning, he

43. A good resource is V. Philips Long, *The Art of Biblical History*, Foundations of Contemporary Interpretation (Grand Rapids, MI: Zondervan, 1994).

commented, “It will help him defend himself if he gets bullied, but even more so, it will help him carry himself so that he does not get bullied in the first place.” I thought this was an insightful comment. Often the very strength that would help you win a battle enables you to avoid the battle altogether.

In line with this, we should never think that avoiding a fight is a sign of weakness. So often, in life and in theology, it is the exact opposite—to avoid a fight takes a deeper and nobler strength than to engage in one.

Doctrinally serious Christians must remember this, particularly when it comes to third-rank doctrines. We should eagerly pursue the kind of theological conviction and strength that is willing not only to fight for the truth but also to *avoid* fighting in order to promote the gospel. This is the best kind of strength.

Conclusion: A Call to Theological Humility

Sometime around AD 410 or 411, a man named Dioscorus wrote to Saint Augustine, inquiring about how to interpret some of Cicero's dialogues. In his response, Augustine spent much energy warning Dioscorus of the vanity of worldly learning, which he called "ignorant knowledge."

Instead, Augustine commended the humility of the gospel, mediated to us through Christ's incarnation. He urged Dioscorus to "construct no other way for . . . grasping and holding the truth" than the way paved for us by Christ. But what does it mean to do theology in the way of Christ? Augustine explained:

> This way is first humility, second humility, third humility, and however often you should ask me I would say the same, not because there are no other precepts to be explained, but if humility does not precede and accompany and follow every good work we do, and if it is not set before us to look upon, and beside us to lean upon, and behind us to fence us in, pride will wrest from our hand any good deed we do while we are in the very act of taking pleasure in it. . . . If you should ask, and as often as you should ask, about the precepts of the Christian religion, my inclination would

> be to answer nothing but humility, unless necessity should force me to say something else.[1]

My deepest hope is that, if this book accomplishes anything, it commends to us the importance of Augustine's warning. In doing theological triage, humility is the first thing, the second thing, and the third thing. It is our constant need, no matter what issue we are facing.

Why Humility Is So Important

One of the pastors I interviewed in preparation for writing this book shared with me a helpful observation. When people approach the leadership of his church with a doctrinal concern, sometimes they do so in an attitude of humility. For instance, they ask questions and are open to considering new information. They don't assume they already possess a perfect understanding of the issues. But others, sadly, articulate theological disagreements without humility or openness. They simply want to criticize and censure and attack with no consideration that their perspective may not be 100 percent accurate.

This pastor observed that this difference—the presence or absence of humility—was generally far more significant than the actual issue at hand for determining a peaceful and fruitful outcome.[2] Even over significant differences, progress was often made when the discussion was approached with humility and charitable dialogue. On the other hand, disagreements over even relatively minor doctrines can cause untold destruction when approached in an attitude of entitlement and dismissiveness.

This observation weighs heavily on me as I write this conclusion and corresponds to a theme of this book: the divisiveness

1. Augustine, "Letter 118, Augustine to Dioscorus," trans. Wilfrid Parsons, in *The Fathers of the Church*, vol. 18 (New York: The Fathers of the Church, 1953), 282.
2. J. A. Medders put this helpful observation to me in a March 2019 interview.

surrounding a doctrine involves not merely its content but also the attitude with which it is held. The greatest impediment to theological triage is not a lack of theological skill or savvy but a lack of humility. A lack of skill can simply be the occasion for growth and learning, but when someone approaches theological disagreement with a self-assured, haughty spirit that has only answers and no questions, conflict becomes virtually inevitable.

Therefore, we must engage those with whom we have theological disagreements with humility, asking questions to make sure we understand, remembering that we don't see things perfectly, and always seeking to grow in understanding where we may have blind spots. Our attitude toward theology should be, and should always remain, like the Old Breton prayer inscribed on a block of wood on John F. Kennedy's desk: "O God, thy sea is so great, and my boat is so small."

Now, it's easy to admit in principle that you have blind spots. But humility will cause this recognition to make a noticeable difference in your actual interactions with people. It will lead to more clarifying questions, more pursuit of common ground, more appreciation of rival concerns, more delay in arriving at judgments.

In life and theology, it is usually not sheer ignorance that causes the most intractable problems but ignorance *about* ignorance: not the unchartered territory but the stuff that is completely off your map. This is one reason why humility is so important. Humility teaches us to navigate life with sensitivity to the distinction between what we don't know and what we don't know that we don't know. This encourages us to engage in theological disagreement with careful listening, a willingness to learn, and openness to receiving new information or adjusting our perspective. Pride makes us stagnant; humility makes us nimble.

Some worry that too much focus on humility will make us wishy-washy. But humility is not the antonym of strength. On the contrary, those who tremble at God's word are those most likely to stand against human opposition. Consider the courage of Martin Luther, who stood upon God's word against the fiercest opposition even though, as a younger priest, he had been so terrified while administering the Mass that he spilled the wine. As Spurgeon described it: "I believe Martin Luther would have faced the infernal fiend himself without a fear; and yet we have his own confession that his knees often knocked together when he stood up to preach."[3]

In Isaiah 66:2, God himself identifies the qualities that he highly regards and commends:

> This is the one to whom I will look:
> he who is humble and contrite in spirit
> and trembles at my word.

In this book I am less concerned with convincing others of the particular judgments I have made and more concerned that, even where we disagree, we do so in a spirit of trembling before the word of God. This attitude is both the ground and goal of theological triage. "If anyone imagines that he knows something, he does not yet know as he ought to know. But if anyone loves God, he is known by God" (1 Cor. 8:2–3).

Humility Is the Way to Unity

Some Christians are eager to defend sound doctrine. Well and good. But is the *unity* of the body of Christ one of those doctrines we jealously guard? As we observed in chapter 1, the

3. Charles Spurgeon, sermon 2071, "Trembling at the Word of the Lord," in *The Complete Works of C. H. Spurgeon*, vol. 35, *Sermons 2062 to 2120* (Cleveland, OH: Pilgrim, 2013), quoted in Steven J. Lawson, *The Heroic Boldness of Martin Luther* (Sanford, FL: Reformation Trust, 2013), 99.

unity of the church is one of the objects of Christ's death (Eph. 2:14). This, as much as anything, is what the New Testament calls us to cherish and uphold. Therefore, our zeal for theology must never exceed our zeal for our actual brothers and sisters in Christ. We must be marked by love. We must, as my dad always puts it, pursue both gospel doctrine and gospel culture.[4]

In the New Testament, humility is the pathway to unity. For instance, Paul's exhortation to the Philippians about "being of the same mind" (Phil. 2:2) is followed by his appeal to "in humility count others more significant than yourselves" (2:3), in imitation of Christ's action toward them in the gospel (2:5–11).

Or consider Paul's appeal to unity in Romans 14. The presenting issue in this chapter is a conflict over Jewish food laws, but the principles Paul invokes could apply to many other issues as well. His overriding concern in this chapter is that the different convictions held by Roman Christians not be a source of division among them. Thus, the "strong" and the "weak" are called to mutual acceptance. Specifically, amid their differences of conscience, Paul calls them to be welcoming (v. 1), not to quarrel (v. 1), not to despise each other (v. 3), and not to pass judgment one another (vv. 3, 13). Paul even calls the Romans to let go of their rights and adjust their practice in order not to violate the conscience of a brother: "If your brother is grieved by what you eat, you are no longer walking in love. By what you eat, do not destroy the one for whom Christ died" (v. 15).

Today, as well, there are plenty of issues over which Christians will be tempted to quarrel, despise each other, and pass judgment on each other. Instead, we must resolve "never to put a stumbling block or hindrance in the way of a brother" (v. 13). Like Paul, we must even be willing to make sacrificial

4. Ray Ortlund, *The Gospel: How the Church Portrays the Beauty of Christ* (Wheaton, IL: Crossway, 2014).

adjustments for the sake of our unity with others in the body of Christ. If maintaining the unity of the body of Christ is not costing you anything—if it doesn't hurt—then you probably are not adjusting enough.

Paul grounds his appeal in Romans 14 in the fact that each person will stand before the judgment seat of Christ: "Why do you pass judgment on your brother? Or you, why do you despise your brother? For we will all stand before the judgment seat of God" (v. 10). This is healthy to remember: we will give an account of our theological speech and conduct, no less than any other area of our life. When we are standing before the throne on judgment day, what battles will we look back on and be proud we fought? I suspect most of our Twitter debates will not be among them.

Friends, the unity of the church was so valuable to Jesus that he *died* for it. If we care about sound theology, let us care about unity as well.

Concluding Practical Advice

As you read this, you may be working through the practical ramifications of theological triage, whether in your job, your church, your denomination, or some other set of relationships. All of us will face these kinds of challenges at some point or another. The reality is that if you think for yourself, you will likely, at some point or another, hold to a different view than is socially convenient. When that happens, what should you do?

First, *be honest*. We must be transparent about our convictions, even if it causes disruption in our vocation, church life, or relationships. Painful as that is, it is not worth searing your conscience by misrepresenting yourself or your views. Some people seem to "adjust" their convictions with every new context. Whatever other nuances may be involved in how you think about representing your views in the context of ordination or employment, the fact remains that lying is sin. Therefore, when a doctrinal statement requires your affirmation "without mental reservation," it means without mental reservation.

Second, *be tactful.* Honesty is not the same as volunteering your views at the earliest possible moment, regardless of context. There are times to be quiet; there are times to answer only the question you are asked. For instance, when you are sharing the gospel with someone, or when you are seeking to build a Christian friendship, there may be topics you don't intentionally bring up in the initial stages of the conversation or relationship. That is not necessarily compromise; it often reflects wisdom.

Third, *be gracious.* Kindness and civility are becoming scarce these days. More and more, outrage is the norm. Therefore, we can testify to the truth of the gospel by speaking with kindness and moderation as we navigate our theological disagreements. Go out of your way to show love and respect to the other person, even when that person infuriates you. Doing theological triage is an opportunity to live out Jesus's words in John 13:35: "By this all people will know that you are my disciples, if you have love for one another."

Finally, *put your trust in the Lord.* God is sovereign over even your doctrinal changes. He is looking out for you. The hairs on your head are all numbered. You can trust him to guide you and take care of you.

When my wife and I were in Chicago for a year of sabbatical and study, we made Psalm 121:3 our theme verse:

> He will not let your foot be moved;
> he who keeps you will not slumber.

Every night before we went to sleep we prayed for God's guidance for where he would deploy us after the year was over, and God answered that prayer. Looking back at my life, I can see how God has been faithful to guide us throughout our doctrinal and denominational changes, and to bring us to a place where we can happily serve.

It is an encouraging and calming thought to remember that God is attentively watching over the path we walk—including our theological migrations! Put your hope in him, be true to your conscience, and he will open the right doors in the right timing.

A Concluding Prayer

> Lord, where we have sinned either by failing to love the truth or by failing to love our brothers and sisters in our disagreements about the truth, forgive us and help us. For those of us who tend to fight too much over theology, help us to remember that you also died for the unity of the church, your precious bride. Give us softer hearts. For those of us who tend to fight too little over theology, help us to feel our need for courage and resilience. Give us stronger backbones. Help us to be people who tremble at your word and therefore ultimately fear no one but you. Lead us toward that healthy, happy balance of adhering to all your teaching while embracing all your people. Amen.

General Index

Scripture Index

THE GOSPEL COALITION

The Gospel Coalition is a fellowship of evangelical churches deeply committed to renewing our faith in the gospel of Christ and to reforming our ministry practices to conform fully to the Scriptures. We have committed ourselves to invigorating churches with new hope and compelling joy based on the promises received by grace alone through faith alone in Christ alone.

We desire to champion the gospel with clarity, compassion, courage, and joy—gladly linking hearts with fellow believers across denominational, ethnic, and class lines. We yearn to work with all who, in addition to embracing our confession and theological vision for ministry, seek the lordship of Christ over the whole of life with unabashed hope in the power of the Holy Spirit to transform individuals, communities, and cultures.

Through its pastoral resources, The Gospel Coalition aims to encourage and equip current and prospective pastors for faithful endurance over a lifetime of ministry in the church. By learning from experienced ministers of different ages, races, and nationalities, we hope to grow together in godly maturity as the Spirit leads us in the way of Jesus Christ.

Join the cause and visit TGC.org for fresh resources that will equip you to love God with all your heart, soul, mind, and strength, and to love your neighbor as yourself.

TGC.org